MADE
★ IN ★
AMERICA

WARNING

If you are easily offended or a politically correct drone, continue no further. Rather, roll this book into a tube, wrap it in sandpaper that has been soaked in battery acid, set it upright, hover your sphincter above, and fucking squat. Repeat until unconscious.

MADE ★ IN ★ AMERICA

GET YOUR 'MERICA ON

JMF THOMAS

Made In America
JMF Thomas

Contact us at jmfthomas@getyourmericaon.com
Follow on Twitter @JMFThomas

ISBN: 978-0-9856763-0-8

Edited by Lynn Cross, Callie Rathburn, and Kendra Zager
Cover Design by Sammantha Langer
Book Layout by Sammantha Langer
Cover Photography by Alex Uncapher

First Edition: January 2013
All stories in this book are as factual as possible. However, any
person, artist, program, event, movie, company, organization,
establishment, entity, or product other than JMF Thomas mentioned
in the Made In America stories, even if based on real life, is fictional.
Reference to anything that can be classified into the previous
categories listed above is an impersonation, parody, or satire done
very inaccurately, and should not be taken seriously or reflect any
real-life counterparts. This book is intended for humor/comedy
and should not be taken seriously or literally. By going forward and
reading this book, you acknowledge and understand the above
statement.

If the previous disclaimer resembles the opening disclaimer on every
South Park episode, it is merely a coincidence, and no language
from the *South Park* disclaimer inspired the previous disclaimer.

This novel is dedicated to all the sisters of my best friends.
May I someday bang all of you.

☆ ☆ ☆

★ ★ ★ TABLE OF CONTENTS

PRELUDE

It's very ironic that I have chosen to write a book because I never read them. The last book I read was *To Kill a Mockingbird* in ninth grade. That book can lick my hairy gooch, and Boo Radley can go fuck himself.

Why would anyone devote their time to reading that shit? Books like that made me SparkNote every required book I had to read from high school through college. If you can pass a test without reading the book, what does that tell you about our school system? No wonder Americans can't count to ten or spell anything without the red squiggly in Microsoft Word. I know I can't. Why read a book when some asshole director in Hollywood will envision it for me? Two hours and a hundred pages in ten fucking minutes. It's simply more efficient. The correct term is "opportunity cost." Microeconomics 103. At least I learned something in business school.

So, if books make me want to deep-throat a chainsaw, then why the fuck am I writing this? Well, hopefully this sells and I won't have to sit in a cube for the rest of my life making Excel spreadsheets. I'd rather be drunk on a yacht pouring Cristal on bitches' titties. Isn't that what everyone wants? Hit it big and become an unproductive socialite? (Patience, Paris Hilton, I will be joining you soon.) I know that's my American dream.

If you purchased this book, I thank you for making my dream come true. If you borrowed it or got it at the library, then you can go fist yourself. Who the hell goes to the library these days? Wikipedia whatever you need to know, idiot. Although I can't really criticize people for pirating. I have a ten-thousand-song library on my hard drive that I paid absolutely nothing for. Sorry, Metallica.

The last album I bought was Nelly's *Country Grammar* in middle school. I was the coolest kid on my bus route, believe dat. You know Nelly's target market was white, suburban, middle-school kids, right? Come to think of it, why am I writing this? Because Nelly taught me, with the chorus of his hit single "Ride Wit Me," that "Hey! It must be the money!" In my case, the proceeds will total ten dollars when my mom, the only consumer, buys my book. Thank you, Mother. I love you. Can you call me up from the basement when dinner is ready?

So basically, I'm writing a book geared toward people who don't read books. It's like I'm trying to sell mirrors to blind people, headphones to deaf people, or swimsuits to black people. Horrible business ventures. I know. I get it. But goddamn it, if they can get Helen Keller to say "wawa," then I can get some Halo geek to get off the couch, put down the sticks, and read a fucking book. No child left behind. You're welcome, Dubya. The thing is, I'd love to sit down and read an entertaining book. But I don't want to read about a Catholic conspiracy, a traveling pair of pants, or especially a self-proclaimed asshole who makes up stories about banging midgets. I want to read something that I can relate to. I want stories of people pissing their pants when they pass out, failing at picking up chicks, and getting arrested when they're too intoxicated to know it. That's the story of my life. Furthermore, I think that the better part of America experiences a similar void, and I hope to fill it.

I've participated in many less-than-intelligent activities, and I hope you get a kick out of some of them. But before you continue reading, if you're a younger cousin, grandparent, or potential future employer, immediately take this book outside, cover it in gasoline, and drop a match on it. As far as you're concerned, this book was about all my summers volunteering as a Bible camp counselor. Thank you for your cooperation. For the rest of you cool kids, let's, without further ado, bring on that sweet, that nasty, and that gushy stuff.

WHITE BOY LAKE

Before we storm the beaches of Normandy, I think a briefing on my background is essential. I don't want you to cruise through this book without knowing that, just so you don't automatically assume I should be wearing a helmet and drool bib.

I was brought into the world when doctors performed a successful cesarean section on my mother in December of 1987. Had my parents consulted Miss Cleo regarding the future of their fetus, my bet is that my pregnant mother would have walked out the door and instantly become a bull rider. But she didn't, and now she's stuck going to bat for me after every idiotic thing I do. Albert Pujols doesn't have shit on my mother. She goes yard every time.

My family raised me in the City of Lakes and Legends, White Bear Lake, Minnesota. The best way to describe White Bear Lake? Go to urbandictionary.com and reference definition #2:

White Bear Lake

1. A suburb of St. Paul, Minnesota, with a population of roughly twenty-five thousand, with 120 percent of that being white.
2. A suburb widely known for vast numbers of white people.
3. See WHITE.

Get the picture? I'm assuming most people reading this book come from a similar background. Don't read too much into the previous sentence, but, in general, people who live in suburbs have higher literacy rates and higher disposable incomes. Thus, suburban residents are more likely to purchase literature than a resident of say, Compton, California. Sorry, Compton, you're just not my target market. The only knowledge I have of cooking crack, slapping chickenheads, and contracting AIDS (RIP, Eazy) is from the time I've invested playing Grand Theft Auto on my sixty-five-inch HDTV.

Just because it's not Compton doesn't mean White Bear Lake doesn't have its own share of dangers and hardships. We have potholes, traffic violators, free-running barking dogs, and sometimes the ice cream shop runs out of your favorite soft serve flavor. Let me tell you, when Cup and Cone runs out of orange and I have to settle for watermelon, it really puts a damper on my day. Stressful.

For eleven years, I was completely content with living in my White Bear Lake bubble. I loved my turn for show and tell when I could bring my kittens into class. I loved going to soccer practice and receiving my participation trophy like everyone else. I especially loved going to the Dairy Queen when my report card had more E's (excellent) than S's (satisfactory). This vanilla life grew mundane when I turned twelve. I had to get out of the burbs, and I knew the only way was to get my hustle on. Get rich or die tryin', right, Fifty?

I hustled everything. I'm talking bottle rockets, Pokemon cards—and *Playboys*. The magazines were the crack epidemic of my middle school. I could get five dollars per page and fifteen for a foldout. I was balling "fo sho." Thanks to my underground business, I had it all: Abercrombie and Fitch clothes (get that Hollister shit out of here), GT BMX bikes equipped with pegs, and three Giga Pets.

But just like when Nancy Reagan started the Just Say No war on drugs campaign and fucked up Compton's drug hustle, the Internet was becoming increasingly more accessible and fucked up my hustle. Naked chicks could be downloaded instantly, and my Playboy Empire came crashing down before my eyes. My only option was to become a gangbanger.

My friends and I had our hood on lock. We ruled our pristine lakefront roads with no mercy. If we caught you slippin', your million dollar house is getting fucked. We would roll fifteen deep and creep up on your house at night while you were sleeping. Your manicured trees would get skeeted up with TP, your Lexus Saran wrapped, and all your decorative garden art would be tipped-the-fuck over. WHAT!

If the next day was recycle day, all the neighborhood bins would be gathered and dumped in your yard. To top it off, a couple rolls of Black Cats would be thrown in your mailbox to light up the motherfucking neighborhood like Afghanistan. No one was more legit than my crew and me. How the History Channel never approached us for an episode of *Gangland* is beyond me. They give time for those wanksta-ass Bloods and Crips? Bitch, please.

Please excuse my language and actions so far. My music of choice growing up was Eminem, Limp Bizkit, Kid Rock, Korn, NWA, Ludacris, and Dr. Dre. My favorite television programs featured Degeneration X, Stone Cold Steve Austin, the Jackass crew, and girls jumping on trampolines every week. Not to mention the character in my favorite video game, who screamed, "GET OVER HERE," before he launched a knife into my opponent's heart and finished him off with an uppercut. WHOOPSIE! So, yeah, maybe all that had something to do with my fascination with reppin' the gangbanger lifestyle in my quaint suburban city.

The gangsta way of life was, and is, a full-time occupation. But even the hardest Gs need to have some fun. And that's where the summer between seventh and eighth grade came into play. After a successful Roman candle assault on an unsuspecting passing car, we headed to my buddy's house for Freeze Pops and lunch. It was the usual routine. We'd hit the couch and try to catch a glimpse of a nipple through the scrambled Spice channel provided by his dad's pirate box. "BOOOOB! I swear I just saw one!" (It was probably a dude's but definitely still a nipple.) My buddy broke off my "Where's Waldo?" boob hunt when he emerged from the kitchen with a bottle of Captain Morgan. Sure, I'll give it a try. Why not? After a sip or two and a fuzzy feeling in my brain, I was sold. This was awesome. From here on out, alcohol was my tiger blood (thanks, Charlie Sheen). The Captain and I did everything together. Controlling our suburban hood lost its allure as more shots were thrown back over the next couple of years.

My attempts at gangbanging and being the real Slim Shady ended entirely once I hit the ninth grade. However, by that point, I had tripled my alcohol consumption like the Twenty-first Amendment had just been ratified. For the next four years, every weekend began with a call to a twenty-five-year-old White Bear High School dropout who was living with his parents and willing to buy alcohol for minors. I was very grateful for this service, but let's be honest, what a fucking loser. The combination of easily accessible alcohol and a whole student body that craved it like Tiger Woods craves kinky hotel romps created a high school experience that made the Jersey Shore look like a party thrown by the Church of Latter Day Saints.

My parents were cool with me getting my party on as long as I had good grades. I could do whatever I wanted if I got all A's and B's. Filling that requirement was not hard in the least. You basically just had to show up to class. (If you can't get at least a C average in public school, then you might as well drop out ASAP and start your career path to chief button presser in a factory line. If you're struggling through high school, I just don't think law school is going to pan out the way you want. Not to be insensitive, but why waste your time, and my tax dollars?) So anyway, while other kids were trying to grasp $a2 + b2 = c2$, I was passed out on a couch with people drawing swastikas and dicks on my face. There's nothing worse than waking up in the morning looking like a Nazi drag queen.

Finding a party was the easy part. Someone's parents were always out of town. If we had to, we would just find a field. One time someone got the brilliant idea to drive our cars onto a golf course and party on the green. That, of course, ended when the cops came a half hour later, and I had to traverse two sand traps and a swamp to reach freedom. Swamps and woods were generally how most of our parties ended. Worth it. I think I could teach Bear Grylls a thing or two about survival. Man vs.Drunk.

The party itself was usually the same every time, too. A bunch of minors would get hammered in a basement trying to recreate the college parties from all of those movies they saw that all had the same plot: try to get laid. The only difference is that McLovin would never come close to getting laid in any of our parties. I was a little higher up than McLovin on the sex food chain, but by no means was I pulling tail like the hockey team. (Non-Minnesnowtans: We have an unofficial caste system where, if you play hockey, you're in the Brahmin, AKA elite, class). The hockey guys were lions. I couldn't just snap my fingers and, abracadabra, get a blowjob in a closet. But hey, every now and then, I, the resourceful hyena, found something left over to bite into. I was completely fine with that. The other 95 percent of the parties when I wasn't biting into something, I had to entertain myself in other ways. I had a couple of options at my disposal.

The first option wasn't so much a choice as it was an inevitability. A fight will break out when you have a bunch of drunk, immature guys in one room. It's like parking your rimmed-out Escalade on 8 Mile Road. It will be on cinder blocks by morning. Fighting wasn't anything new. I got in a couple of scuffles here and there throughout high school, always over the dumbest shit. I'd have to say, my most memorable throw-down happened over nothing.

I was at a party and got a call that So-and-So wanted to fight me. Not wanting to be a pussy, I drove to his house with my friends and stood in his yard yelling, "Come at me, Brah!" The guy stumbled out, shitfaced, and we started duking it out in the street. We were so drunk we probably looked like two retards playing tag in the dark. After about ten minutes, his mother and younger brother ran out, with her screaming, "Go get the gun!" The younger brother bolted back inside the house. At that point, going up unarmed against a small militia made my odds for victory less probable. Can you say Hotel Rwanda?

My friends grabbed me, and we scampered back to the car as the guy continued to punch me in the back of the head. I have a big-ass head, so hitting it is easier than landing in water if you jumped out of a boat. We peeled the fuck out of there. I wish Ron Burgundy had been there because that escalated really quickly.

If the threat of having a piece of lead lodged in your body isn't for you, then there is always another way to pass the time at parties. The next option is more fluffy and lighthearted. You can pull a prank on the host's house. Some guys would pull pranks that were too obvious. For example, one time a few guys put paper towels in the upstairs bathroom sink, and it flooded the room below. In this house, the bathroom was located right above the dining room. I was sitting at the table, and a stream of water began pouring out from the chandelier. Funny, yes. But also distasteful. I preferred subtle pranks that no one would notice at the time and wouldn't cause damage.

I would simply switch objects between rooms. It could be a painting switched with a clock. Or it could be chairs rearranged in a particular room. When the host cleaned up the next day before his or her parents got home, the kid wouldn't notice the switch. But you knew for damn sure that the mother would come home and ask, "Why is the family portrait on the opposite wall?" The following Monday the host would come to school all bewildered and say, "I cleaned up all evidence of the party, but I still got caught because some idiot switched the cookie jar with the microwave, and now I'm grounded." Ha ha. That was me. Dipshit.

Now believe me, I understand that getting caught for throwing a party while your parents are gone is never a fun experience. One night, I had a colossus of a party at my house. I don't remember much from that evening, but the one image that will forever be etched into the hard drive of my brain is the abundance of high school girls partying completely naked in my hot tub. (The best part about that memory is that even though I keep getting older, that image stays the same age. Allllriiiight.) So, come Sunday morning, it was cleanup time. I picked up all the cans, conscientiously refilled my parents' alcohol bottles with water, and got all the couches and chairs back to their appropriate positions. Sunday night my parents came home and didn't suspect a thing. It was perfect.

I was sitting in the living room when my dad decided to unwind in the hot tub. All I heard was, "WHAT THE FUCK!!!" Shit, the one place I didn't check. He stormed up to me yelling, "THERE'S A FUCKING CONDOM FLOATING IN THE HOT TUB!" FML. Busted. My parents were livid. They drained the hot tub and made me scrub out the entire thing with a toothbrush. I found this punishment both cruel and unusual. It violated my Eighth Amendment rights. But at this point, my house had become a colony of North Korea and I no longer had any rights. I was grounded for a month.

If for some reason we couldn't get a party going in the burbs, there was always the backup plan. Hit up a club. In the Twin Cities, there are sixteen-plus dance clubs sprinkled generously throughout the area. The gross part is that the age cutoff for these clubs is twenty-five. That's statutory rape, brotha. At any rate, it's a great place to meet peers from neighboring communities. And by that I mean, clubs are great places for a suburban guy to meet all the inner-city hood rat chicks who are more than willing to get some internship experience for their future careers of selling companionship on Craigslist.

You always felt cool going to the club. You got to act out all the rap videos you saw on BET. But every rap video is in slow motion, and I quickly learned that's not as cool when you do it in real life. Chicks don't find sloths hot. Despite that misconception, we would roll up in my buddy's Escalade with its twenty-inch spinners. All of the hood rats would flock to it and shake, drop, and twerk their asses, with the rims as backdrops, like the vixens in hip-hop videos. Make that ass roll, girl. You could see the dollar signs in their eyes reflecting off their dreams of monthly child support checks. It was like shooting fish in a barrel.

You had to be careful with those girls. They were the type of girls who would poke a hole in the condom to get knocked up so they wouldn't have to do shit for the rest of their life. We've all watched the show *16 and Pregnant*. You couldn't blame them; they were just following the footsteps of their families, the role model of the single mother who sits on her ass all day waiting for her government check, father nowhere to be found. The apple doesn't fall far from the tree.

One night, my buddy D-Black met a girl at one of the clubs, and we decided to meet up with her and her friends the next day. We pulled up to a ghetto-ass house in the inner city. It was sketchy. I swore I'd seen that house on *Cops* on more than one occasion. When we knocked on the door, her drunk-ass dad answered and immediately started on a profanity-laced rant about why we were at his home. I'm assuming he thought we were sent by his meth dealer to collect his drug debt. That should have been our cue to leave, but D-Black had poontang on his brain.

We finally convinced the dad we were legit, and he let us in. We were hanging out in the basement with the girls when I noticed something that looked like a hospital bracelet. I asked the girl who was in the hospital. She laughed and said, "No, that's my dad's bracelet from prison; he just got out." Well, isn't that just fucking great. D-Black and the girl then went into the next room to get freaky. Twenty minutes later, I heard the dad upstairs screaming for us to leave. He had finally figured out we were there to bang his daughter and didn't find that too amusing. I frantically knocked on the door where D-Black was still with the girl. The felony-convicted father started yelling that he was getting his shotgun and would blow our heads off. D-Black and the girl ran out of the room. The look on her face said it all: Her dad had done this before. All I could think was, maybe this is why he was in prison, shooting two idiots trying to bang his daughter. We scrambled past him before he even had time to take aim.

We made it home safely. It did raise my adrenalin level, but I can't say that I really miss my times in the ghetto. I'll just stick to watching *Training Day* in the comfort of my home.

The one thing I do miss about high school is my immunity to hangovers. I could be out till two in the morning drinking, wake up at 6:00 a.m., and, within an hour, be at football practice running sprints in eighty-degree summer heat.

Oddly, I never really cared about football. I never saw the field. I was Radio minus the Down syndrome. I will, however, confidently say that I was the best at running laps on the team. I'd always be goofing off on the sidelines, but when coach would casually say, "Thomas. Laps," it was YES, SIR. That was my moment to shine. Without hesitation, I'd gracefully run the two hundred yards to my fence and back.

During the games, I'd pray that the coach wouldn't put me in. I wore so many layers under my pads that my mobility was comparable to that of a little kid in a snowsuit. Lay off, it's fucking cold standing there for three hours. I kept a pack of Skittles and can of chew under my thigh pads, for Christ's sake. Every game while I stood on the sidelines, my friends in the stands would chant, "PUT. IN. THOM-AS." Coach, give the people what they paid to see.

They finally got their wish when we were in the playoffs against some shitty inner-city team during the first round. We were up 31-0 when the chant started, and coach turned around and told me to get in. Goddamnit, Coach. I'm enjoying my Gatorade right now. But my fans needed me. I took my giant mittens off and ran onto the field to man the strong safety position.

(Ladies and gay guys, I know I'm losing you at this point. Let me help you out. Strong safety is on defense. Defense stops the other team from scoring points. The more your defense keeps the other team's offense from scoring, the more likely you will win the game. You probably won't understand the next couple of paragraphs involving football terminology. That's okay. I'm sorry, but I'm not going to dumb it down for you. Go make yourself an orange mocha frappuccino and resume reading in three paragraphs.)

No one believes me, but to this day, I still feel like the other team had the momentum and was about to stage a comeback despite the thirty-one-point deficit. They were on their forty-yard line and putting together a nice drive. The QB hiked the ball, and I read run. I ran up five yards before I realized it was pass. Fuck, I'm burned.

The QB launched the ball down the middle of the field to the open receiver streaking down the middle of my zone. The QB threw such a duck that I was able to run back and pick it off. All I saw was open field. My immediate thoughts were Ochocinco and end zone dance. I'd never been to the end zone, and there was no way I was passing up my one chance to moonwalk and spike that fucking ball, regardless of a fifteen-yard unsportsmanlike-conduct penalty. But, of course, my true athletic ability shone through, and I tripped over my own feet and ate shit.

Whatever, I still halted the comeback and crushed all our opponent's momentum. The crowd chanted, "WE. LOVE. THOM-AS." I saluted them all as I walked off the field, having played the last down of my football career. I think I still hold the school record for 100 percent of passes thrown my way ending in an interception. Troy Polamalu can't say that, and he's an MVP in the NFL. I'll hang my hat on that. I think we ended up losing the next game. Who cares? Finally, the season was over, and my only commitment for the rest of my senior year, which I faithfully kept, was parties.

Well, there it is. I think this is an appropriate time for me to say, "Hi. My name's Mr. Thomas, and I like to party." Ever since middle school, I've had a knack for letting mischief find me. Almost every weekend night since the ninth grade I've gone out and killed a case of beer. One of the "Good Ol' Boys." My only memories of growing up are vandalizing houses, attending parties, and not caring about anything in the world. I'm in my element when I have a group of friends and a bottle of whiskey in my hand. I wasn't a bad kid; I just liked to have fun.

Ninety percent of the time, the parties and experiences were the same every weekend, and I did not really distinguish myself all that much, in the beginning, from my peers. But as time has passed, I've come to recognize and appreciate the unique predicaments I find myself getting into. There is a long string of events that have happened to me that not too many other people can say they have experienced. And the string started in Puerto Vallarta, Mexico, at the end of my senior year of high school.

PARTY VALLARTA, PART UNO

I like to think of North America as a family. America, Mexico, and Canada have unique relationships with one another. I relish the opportunity for the three family members to get together. In my experiences, these family reunions usually border on the weird/incestuous side. I'm cool with that.

Mexico is like the uncle who the family is not proud of. They don't like to mention his name at family gatherings, and he probably has several prison stints on his record. But he's still your favorite uncle because he's the go-to guy for a party. You'd never want to live at his house because it reeks of urine and poop, but if you want to get away from reality, he'll let you throw a party on his property for a weekend.

Anything goes at Uncle Mexico's house. Underage girls, illicit drug use, and donkey shows are par for the course. Nothing is too outrageous for Uncle Mexico. Anything that you've done, Uncle Mexico did it high on cocaine with three dead strippers in the trunk of his car on his Monday morning commute while casually sipping a coffee. Whenever I'm at Uncle Mexico's house, I can do whatever the hell I want, and that's why I love him.

Now Canada, on the other hand, is like your cousin. The one you never think about. He lives way out in the middle of nowhere, and that's why you never hear about him. At all the family gatherings, Cousin Canada just sits there. Don't get me wrong, Cousin Canada is a very polite and respectful young man. But let's just say you aren't too thrilled when, after the family get-together, your mother makes you let Cousin Canada tag along with you to the bar. No one likes going out with their lame cousin.

So anyway, when you get to the bar, Cousin Canada starts downing a bottle of whiskey like it's water. Goddamn. I should've been hanging out with this son of a bitch a lot sooner. Before you can finish that thought, Canada is on the bar, pouring shots down everyone's throat and lighting up a doobie. All of a sudden, you feel like the lame ass as you struggle to finish your American light beer. At last call, Canada is leaving with two hotties for a threesome, and you're left by yourself to pull your own pork for the rest of the night. Who knew?

The ultimate family reunion is when you and Cousin Canada get to throw a party at Uncle Mexico's house. That's exactly the situation I was fortunate enough to encounter on my senior spring break in Puerto Vallarta. That trip was the best week of my life. It's like I took every immoral thing in the world and blended it into a delicious smoothie. I drank that smoothie every day. It tasted like vagina, weed, beer, and butthole. I could write an entire book from that week. But since Americans have the attention span of a kid with ADD, I'll just give you a couple of chapters.

I was with my best friend Tom (AKA The Dirty Afghan). He isn't really Afghan, but his tan skin, questionable hygiene, and low standards for women closely resemble those of a terrorist. Tom is the type of guy who settles for the first female who talks to him at the bar. It doesn't matter if she's fat, skinny, old, young, has three kids, or is in a wheelchair. If she's remotely interested, he's interested. I can't tell you how many times I've woken up in the same room as Tom and looked over to see him being cuddled by Shrek. The women he brings back to the hotel room defy the laws of physics. How they haven't broken his dick off should be investigated by the scientific community. He's the perfect person to bring to a dirty place like Puerto Vallarta.

Upon our arrival at our hotel, Tom and I headed to the all-inclusive bar by the pool like the blitzkrieg into Belgium. There we met some dudes from Vancouver, who quickly took us under their wing. Let the North American family reunion commence. Cousin Canada showed us what a day at Uncle Mexico's house is all about.

We started by taking tequila shots with the moose fuckers. Trying to keep pace with them was mistake number one. Canadians must be bottle fed with whiskey as babies. It was like trying to compete against Blake Griffin in a dunk contest. I couldn't even touch the net.

As if being shitfaced wasn't enough, we then went up to the Canadians' room, and they were all doing lines of booger sugar off the table. I declined the cocaine offer. That stupid DARE lion from high school was in the back of my mind telling me, "Don't. You better not." I listened, but that didn't keep me from getting high as fuck on the balcony from some sticky icky. After we had all elevated our mental states, the Canadians wanted to go back to the bar to meet some girls. If I seem like I'm rushing through the story, I'm not. This is the actual pace. I should be dead right now.

When we got back down to the hotel bar, it was time to start engaging in the best part of spring break: the women. Spring break is great because only hot girls head to beaches then. Fat girls are too self-conscious for beaches, thank God. Their spring breaks consist of missionary trips building houses in Nicaragua. Basically anywhere they don't have to show skin. Good riddance. This was great news for me. If only hot chicks are around, it raises the average hotress standard. A girl at the bar that is normally a 9 becomes a 6 on spring break due to the oversaturation of hotties. That puts her in my ballpark, which sucks for her—once you enter my ballpark, the door locks behind you.

After spring break, you will never see these girls again. I like to have alter egos when I talk to girls like that. Sometimes my name is Garrett Ramfelt from New York and I trade stocks on Wall Street. Or maybe Rusty Walker from Texas and I work at a rodeo. I don't do it to impress the girls. I do it in case of unplanned consequences. She will be looking for the daddy in Brooklyn or Houston rather than Minneapolis. It's quite possible there are some little curly-haired Thomases or Thomasinas running around somewhere out there. I want you little fuckers to contact me only if you become rich and famous. Otherwise, good luck with life, my offspring.

So there I was with the Canadians, scanning the beach for the drunkest girl, the one spitting mouthfuls of sand from repeatedly falling over, or attempting to put her shirt on as pants. I thought Tom was right beside me surveying the beach. He was not. I looked over and saw him chatting up a fortysomething woman at the bar. Really? We are at a high-dollar steakhouse, and he just ordered a salad? I wasn't surprised. Like I said, first vagina to interact with him, and he's sold. Game over.

I will be the first to say that it's every man's dream to catch a cougar. It's a great addition to your sex résumé. But just because the woman is a cougar doesn't mean she's a MILF. Tom's selection was far from MILF status. She looked like she was Rampage Jackson's punching bag. That "MILF" was a hideous human specimen. Perfect for Tom.

As I watched Tom, the Canadians had already corralled a collection of cuties from the beach and were laying their game on thick. That was irrelevant to me because I couldn't keep my eyes off the imminent car crash with Tom and the "MILF." I knew impact was near when she climbed up on the bar screaming, "Whooooo, body shots, whoooo!" The only person who shared her enthusiasm was Tom. All the other patrons around the bar looked like they were watching Cupchicks for the first time. (Why is that cup there? Wait, oh my god, no! She did not just shit in that. What the fuck?)

To be fair, it wasn't that this lady was fat. She was skinny. But she had the loose skin of a gastric bypass patient. I think saggy skin is worse than when you have a girl whose weight scale screams, "Get the fuck off me. I can't breathe," every time she steps on it. A good friend would have pulled Tom's drunk ass away from the death sentence of taking a body shot off this withered beast. I was not that good friend.

The bartender, who looked like he had just seen Rosie O'Donnell's butthole, reluctantly began pouring tequila onto the lady's belly button. I was actually a little nervous when they put the salt on her. Her leathery skin needed only another tablespoon of salt to become beef jerky. Once the lime was placed in her mouth, Tom's tongue went to work.

I give him props. If it were me, I would have opted for dipping my tongue in a wood chipper. But Tom slurped up every bit of salt and flaked skin that he could, and then ventured to the tequila-filled belly button abyss. He suctioned it out like a leech and spit that shit out of there like a Jell-o shot. I say Jell-o shot because I'm sure whatever called that belly button home had curdled that tequila into a semi-solid state. He then elegantly yanked the lime from her lips and put his hands in the air as if he had just won a marathon. (I know his tongue must have felt that way.)

She popped up from the bar and swung her legs around him like a bear trap. Tom didn't attempt to escape her mighty grasp. He simply accepted his fate like a wounded fawn. The expressions of the people around the bar at this point were priceless. It was like when Ace Ventura popped out of the rhino's ass. It's safe to say my face was like the little boy's. COOOL!

After a couple minutes of tongue hockey, they romantically held hands and walked toward the rooms. And by romantic, I mean "dragging her fresh kill back to her cave to have her way with him." I was faced with a serious dilemma. On one hand, I could have let them go and, yes, that would have made for an even better story. However, the odds that this old bag had contracted something during her wild, unprotected sexual endeavors of the '80s were probable. Did they even use condoms back then?

In good conscience I couldn't let my best friend wake up in the morning tied to a hotel bed in Mexico with a glaze of forty-year-old oyster spunk dried on his face and half his penis gone. So I chose the latter option and decided to save my best friend. My reasoning was simple. The Canadians had a crew of hot college girls ready to do squats on any guy who was willing to give them a spot. I'd take that over the Medusa that Tom was about to get raided by any day of the week.

I thought I could just walk up to the couple, pull him away, and we'd be back with the hotties in no time. But no, she clamped down on him like a pit bull. Fortunately, my years of investing in protein powders finally paid a dividend, and after an extended and bruising tug of war, her slithery hands finally gave way. But when I tried to tell Tom about the girls the Canadians had rounded up, he just gave me a blank stare. If Tom can't rally for vagina, it's nappy time. His ungrateful drunk ass didn't even thank me for my valiant rescue. Instead, he called me a fag and passed in and out of consciousness as I hoofed him up the four flights of stairs to our room. I threw his ass on the bed, and he puked all over it.

I spent the rest of the day in the bar hanging out with the Canucks and the college girls. I ended up hooking up with a redhead, and she was my first, and last, ginger. I know some guys think all the freckles on a ginger are cute. I do not. I think they are confusing. When you take a ginger's shirt off, you see a million dots. Which two dots are her nipples? I'm just not attracted to a girl who looks like she's been splattered with paint. That belongs in an art gallery, not my bedroom.

After the ginger, I tried my damndest to represent America by partying all night with the Canadians. But I felt like I had let my country down by passing out on a toilet at 10:00 p.m. while taking a shit at a bar. There's nothing better than coming through to your pants down on a Mexican toilet with puke dried to the side of your mouth. (Note: I like how you can use Mexican as an adjective in front of any noun and it immediately turns that noun dirty.)

In my defense, one of the Canadians gave me a chew to throw in my lip, which I gutted, thus immediately banishing me to the bathroom for the rest of the night. Even though my night came to an abrupt end, I still thank God that I was able to have the North American family reunion. Cousin Canada gave me the blueprint for a successful week at Uncle Mexico's house. I am forever in debt to him.

Our first day in Mexico pretty much foreshadowed the daily routine for the remainder of our week. You wake up and smell your fingers from the girl last night, go to the tiki bar, drink, try to hit on chicks, get rejected, drink, smoke weed, drink, maybe eat, drink, ward off the locals bombarding you to buy shit they probably stole out of your hotel room, drink, stumble to the bars/clubs, drink, try to pick up chicks, drink, try to sneak the non-hotel-guest chicks past hotel security, fail, drink, try to bang the same hotel guest-chicks from the night before (gross), and pass out nowhere close to your bed. It never got old. However, every now and then, Uncle Mexico would throw you a curve ball just to see how you react. He thought it was funny. I thought it was cruel, and for that, he won't be receiving a present at Navidad time from me.

PARTY VALLARTA, PART DOS

Uncle Mexico pitches one hell of a game. He starts by throwing the same pitch over and over. Then all of a sudden he lofts an underhand pitch and lets you bang one out of the park. Notice how I used the word bang. Don't be fooled by how easy that underhand pitch was to hit. Uncle Mexico is just toying with you. Just when you think you have Uncle Mexico's strategy figured out, he throws a 110-mile-per-hour heater straight to your fucking dome. Tom and I started the day off like any other day—drinking and creeping out chicks. It didn't bother us that our game wasn't working anymore. These girls were from our hotel. Been there, done that. It's like bubble wrap. Once you pop the bubbles, there's no point anymore. So we just drank the day out until it was time to go to the clubs.

The bars/clubs are the lofted underhand pitch by Uncle Mexico. You better hit that home run, homeboy. The bars themselves are the ultimate wingman. And the best part is that the girls aren't even aware of the wingman's presence. It's like *Angels in the Outfield*. Remember that movie? The Angels' baseball team won all their games because invisible angels were interfering with the other team's players on the field, causing them to fuck up.

That's exactly what the clubs do for you in Mexico. They help you win. Do you think the girls would be taking their shirts off in the middle of a public place if they weren't in that bar? Of course not. Soon as they walk in that bar, those angels fly on over and tear that bra off. Then an angel guides her hand down your pants and takes you to heaven. There's no other way to explain it. Angels in Da Club.

Tom and I chose, as our first bar of the evening, one of the generic bars that are in every Mexican spring break city. It was probably Señor Frog's or Carlos O'Brian's. Does it really matter? All of those bars are the same damn thing. Loud rave music with a bunch of dipshits blowing whistles in your ear. Whatever. The main thing was, they were having a wet t-shirt contest. Who ever invented that contest deserves a Nobel Peace Prize. That award is given to individuals who have made a difference in the world. To me, that guy has made the biggest difference in the world. He's my hero.

With the girls assembling on the stage, Tom and I plowed through the crowd to get front row. (On a side note, I don't understand why it's called a wet t-shirt contest. All the girls are wearing the same white t-shirts, with no bra, and they all get sprayed with water. Where's the contest? By the title of the contest, you would assume the winner is the little angel who has the wettest t-shirt. How would you judge that? I'm assuming they could maybe wring out the t-shirts into a bucket and declare the winner by who has the largest volume of water. I'm glad they don't do that. That would mean the heftier girls with the larger-sized shirts would always win. Gross. No one needs to see those stretch marks. It's also a safety hazard for everyone at the bar if that much weight is on stage. We don't need another Sugarland. I'm all about safety first. No fatties.)

In reality, the winner of the wet t-shirt contest is the girl who takes off the most clothing and dances the sluttiest on stage in front of a crowd of strangers, all of whom are carrying camera phones that have 4G capability, meaning the photos can be instantly uploaded to the Internet. Hey, Toby Keith, what happens down in Mexico doesn't necessarily stay in Mexico. I am by no means complaining about the amateur strip competition. I just find it funny that giving it a cute name somehow registers in a girl's brain that it isn't slutty. Stupid girls. That's why we love you so much.

Anyway, Tom and I loved every minute. As planned, the winner of the contest was the lovely young lady who got completely naked and did this weird handstand maneuver where she propped her feet onto the wall and danced upside down. It was a beautiful, well-deserved victory. Her routine combined grace, creativity, and a high level of difficulty. If anyone else had won that t-shirt and two free shots, I would have been thoroughly disappointed in the judges and our society as a whole.

The contest was nice, but you can only look at art for so long. I'd rather fuck the art. We left that bar and headed to a giant club that was having a foam party. This club was one of those clubs that overdoes it on the theatrics. Yes, the people coming down from the ceiling on ropes breathing fire were cool, but if I want to see a show, I'll go to Vegas. The only reason I'm at this club is for the women. And believe me, it had a surplus. Just like in economics, when supply is greater than demand, the price of the product drops. The girls were basically trying to give their vaginas away. I'm all about liquidation prices.

To seal the deal, you basically only had to meet one requirement: your age. Our plan was always to say we were juniors in college. We figured that way we covered all our bases. We could play the cool, older guy card with high school girls and not turn off the college girls by coming off as high school dipshits.

We learned that lesson the first night in Puerto Vallarta when I told one college girl that I was in high school. She responded by pinching my cheek and saying, "Awwww, you're just a li'l guppy." Being equated to Flounder from *The Little Mermaid* does not get you any action. Our revised résumés were simple; I was pre-law at the University of Wisconsin, and Tom was a business major at the University of Minnesota. We were brothers on spring break together. For some reason, saying we were brothers intrigued women. Maybe girls like getting pig roasted. Who knows?

Our stories ended up working on a group of college girls from New Jersey. I mean, they're Jersey girls, so automatically that means they're easy. We were talking their ears off and taking shots for quite some time when like clockwork, the booze hit the girls' brains and they got that urge to dance. They grabbed us by the hands and led us onto the dance floor to "beat that beat up."

(On an unrelated note, I don't think "dance floor" should be the term used anymore. In modern bars, there's not really any dancing that goes on. Have you ever seen a couple break out into the samba or tango? No. All that happens is a lot of grinding and feeling chicks up. It should be called what it is: a petting zoo, a petting zoo where all the animals are boobies and asses.)

When we got to the petting zoo, Lil Jon or the Ying Yang Twins would be blasting over the speakers telling us to "Get low" or "Shake it like a salt shaker." But being white, I resorted to the default form of modern dancing. I positioned myself behind the Guidette, planted my feet like they were in wet concrete, and awkwardly moved my hips as she was in front of me twerking it.

It's really not that bad of a deal. A girl rubs her ass up and down on my dick, and I just stand there trying to not get a full hard-on and stab her in the back. I'd say my generation got this one right. Could you imagine growing up in the twenties and having to swing dance in a ballroom? Fuck that shit.

No guy actually enjoys dancing. The only reason you stand there for so long is either in hopes she comes home with you at bar time, or maybe you get a hand job on the dance floor. Either way, you're going to stand there for four hours, or have your boxers stuck to your leg for the rest of the night. Right when I was about to call it quits on "dancing," the DJ got over the mic and started the countdown for the foam party. Everyone got wet in their pants. It was like the ball dropping on New Year's. Cinco, cuatro, tres, dos, UUUUNNNNNOOO!

And with that, foam fell from the ceiling onto everyone on the floor. On stage, they had giant foam cannons spraying out into the crowd. The place erupted like Mount St. Helens. Within minutes, we were waist-deep in foam. The Guidette started dropping it like it was hot. Who would have ever guessed that bubbles turn girls into Jenna Jameson? How could this get any better?

Well, that question was answered pretty quickly. As I was surveying the crowd, I felt a hand down the front of my pants. I looked down, and the girl was staring up at me grinning. She started unbuckling my shorts belt, and immediately the blood started flowing to my joystick. She grabbed on to the joystick and moved it around like she was steering Yoshi on Rainbow Road in Mario Kart. (I use the Mario Kart reference because we all know that is the only video game that women have the dexterity to play.)

At that point, I was kind of thinking, Right here? In the middle of a dance floor with hundreds of people around me? Who the fuck is this girl? But then it hit me, that's the magic of the foam. No one knows what's going on below foam level. It's the iceberg effect. The concept is genius. So, being a fairly quick learner, I decided to return the favor and play vagina DJ. She was all for it, and I began spinning records.

With both of us colonizing each other, we were both getting pretty horned up. I casually mentioned to her that she was wearing a skirt. She knew exactly what I was getting at and didn't say a word. Rather, she got a smile on her face and pulled her hand out of my pants. She did some adjusting, and when her hand emerged from the foam, she was holding her thong. She then tossed it over her head into the crowd. I'm still thinking, this is not real. But she leaped up and my hands fastened to her thighs.

Her hand went down and politely introduced our parts: Hi, V, meet P. The two quickly became friends and decided to play a game of catch. Yup, this was definitely real, and definitely warm. (Foam makes an excellent lube. I highly recommend it.) We proceeded to "play catch," and that lasted for about one minute. Not because I added my own foam to the party, but because it's quite fatiguing to hold someone up like that. Let's just say she was more body type Snooki than Marisa Miller. She was one of those girls who has a round midsection but really skinny limbs, kind of like the little green eyeball thing in *Monsters, Inc.* Let's be honest, you can't expect a classy, high-quality chick when she's ready for action at a foam party with a complete stranger in Mexico. Exhausted, I put the little bowling ball down, and we just stood there awkwardly.

Part of the awkwardness was from me trying to corral my snake back into its cage. The other part was that she was waiting around for me to make a move and kept trying to hold my hand. Insert Vince Vaughn: we got a stage 5 clinger. I stammered out my best escape plan—I told her I had to poop super bad. Girls hate pooping. She gave me a disgusted, "Did I seriously just have sex with you?" look. I just turned and trotted toward the bathroom clutching my butt to add a touch of realism. For the next couple hours, the plan was to simply avoid the clinger.

By the end of the foam session, it was pretty disgusting. We were standing in an ankle-deep floor cocktail, probably two parts soapy water, one part beer, and one part sex juice. How my feet didn't get encrusted with herpes like barnacles on a ship is still a mystery. If you looked closely throughout the crowd, you could see dudes tucking their junk back in their pants. If there's any silver lining, at least my sexcapade was at the initial foam drop, making me a conductor on that hoe train. You know some of those guys were the caboose of whatever choo choo some of those girls rode that night. At that point, the sanitary level was a bit too low even for me, and I decided to call it a night.

I walked home feeling pretty awesome. I had banged a chick in the middle of a foam party. I am so cool. Uncle Mexico had lofted me a pitch, and I had nailed that fucker out of the park. I was on cloud nine. But like I mentioned earlier, Uncle Mexico was about to pitch me a fastball straight to my head.

PARTY VALLARTA, PART TRES

When Uncle Mexico feels like taking you out of the game, he doesn't fuck around. If you're lucky, your injury won't be career ending, i.e., death, imprisonment, or herpes. I'm now thankful that I was only taken out of the game.

You already know what I was doing all day long. Drinking. Drinking is like my constant variable in a science experiment. I'd tell you what my science experiment was, but I can't remember because of my constant variable. I'm assuming I probably cured cancer. So, after curing cancer all day long, Tom and I once again hit up the bars. We decided to go to a smaller bar instead of a giant club.

A group of girls were sitting at the bar when we walked through the door. One of them instantly caught my attention—she was stunningly beautiful. It was like one of those slow motion scenes in a movie where she had a beam of light around her. We locked eyes. I went over and started talking to her. We chatted all night long. She was a high school senior from Indiana. Her name was Elizabeth. (I still remember it. That's how enchanted I was by her.) It was probably the alcohol, but I was in love. Eventually, we started making out, and around 2:00 a.m., decided to leave the bar together.

Trying to be romantic, I suggested we walk along the beach back to the hotel. HUGE MISTAKE. We held hands like any young couple in love as we walked barefoot in the sand. The ocean was gently crashing onto the shore. The moonlight glistened off her hair. (Totally gay, I know.) We arrived at my hotel, but rather than trying to sneak her by hotel security, we just found a lawn chair on the beach and amped up our making out. Body fluids weren't exchanged, but there was definitely some exploring going on. Fingers may or may not have trespassed into special areas. We lay on the chair for a while and watched the stars in the dark sky. (Also gay, I know.) Eventually, she said that she should get back to her hotel. I agreed to walk her home. As we meandered down the beach, we noticed two guys in the distance coming out of an alley toward us. The moonlight glinted vividly off the rifle one of the guys was carrying. Instantly, being the only two Americans on a dark beach in Mexico didn't seem like the most romantic, or best, place to be. We froze, hoping they hadn't seen us. There was really no place to run. It was flee into the ocean or make a dash on the beach to nowhere in particular. Either way, our intoxicated bodies weren't going to make it very far. Then one of the men yelled out, !ven aca!

My immediate thought was, Oh, fuck my shithole sideways. My second thought was, we're getting robbed, killed, raped, and thrown in the ocean (not necessarily in that order). Best case scenario: we survive and I get on an episode of *Locked Up Abroad*. Elizabeth was freaking out. I told her to be calm and that everything was fine. That was a lie. They continued to yell for us to come over to them. Fuck that. That's like asking me to waltz on over to the gas chamber.

I knew very basic Spanish from my three years of it in high school. But who actually learns a language in high school? Everyone just goes to freetranslation. com for every paper and speech. I had a buddy in my class who wrote his entire Spanish paper on that site. It was 100 percent correct factually, but he translated it into Portuguese and got an F. The point I'm trying to make is that the Spanish I was yelling back to the men was probably really Portuguese and didn't make any sense because I hadn't learned anything in class.

Finally, they cut the bullshit and shouted !policia! Police? Elizabeth and I both looked at each other in relief. I mean, the police are the good guys, right? They're probably just making sure we are enjoying our time in Mexico. They're looking after us. I convinced her that we shouldn't make a dash for it and that we should end the standoff by calmly strolling the last hundred yards over to the policia. When we got close enough, they put up their palms, signaling us to stop. That wasn't the most welcoming gesture. These guys were all business. Stern expressions. One was a fat middle-aged Mexican wearing a cop uniform. The other was a jacked twenty-year-old in military fatigues and holding a military-issue rifle. I'm no gun fanatic, but that rifle looked eerily similar to the ones I use in Call of Duty on Xbox Live to do work on all the elementary school kids.

They started rambling at us a million words a minute. I was trying to talk to them in English, and they had no idea what I was saying. Idiots. I could recognize words here and there, finally figuring out they were saying that it was illegal to be on the beach at night. Well, I'm sorry about that. No one informed me of that rule. Eventually, it seemed like everything was fine, and they were going to let us go home.

As they were escorting us down the alley toward the street, the fat fucker grabbed my arm and pushed me into a smaller, darker alley off the main alley. I thought that was kind of rude. Before I knew what was going on, I was bum-rushed toward their truck and slammed onto the hood. Shit was getting real. The fat fuck spun me around, and all I could see was the barrel of the military guy's rifle pointing at my head.

Now I'm in deep shit. I pictured myself being someone's girlfriend in a Mexican prison. My white, eighteen-year-old American ass and my luscious curly locks inside a Mexican prison would render me zero chance of survival. The second I stepped in there I would be raped, cut, and then traded for a carton of Marlboros. That was going to be the rest of my life—sexual cigarette currency.

The fat fuck began to search me, I'm assuming for drugs, while the military guy kept his rifle aimed at my head. Thank God I didn't have any on me. He was very aggressive with his search, which soon turned inappropriate. I always thought having a middle-aged man touch my butthole would be about as bad as it gets. But it's not. It's having a middle-aged man fondle my butthole in a dark Mexican alley while his friend holds a gun to my head. In the end, he found nothing but my driver's license and like two hundred pesos.

I think these officers were sexist or gay because Elizabeth received none of this treatment. And yet, she was crying and shaking uncontrollably. Maybe she was menstruating. I don't know. I, on the other hand, was remarkably calm. Then came the interrogation, for half an hour, all in Spanish, with that son-of-a-bitch military guy pointing his rifle at my cabeza the whole time.

The officers were getting very frustrated with my inability to answer their questions. (From now on, I think I am going to take it a little bit easier on my amigos at the McDonald's drive-thru when they fuck up my order.) Eventually, the two officers turned their backs on us and began whispering to each other. When they turned back around, they began to negotiate with me like I was Elizabeth's pimp—and in perfect English. They said I could go, but she had to stay. I was flabbergasted. These cocksuckers had understood every goddamn word we were saying the whole time. There was no way I was going to abandon this girl. I couldn't live with myself if I got back to the States and turned the news on to see there had been a Natalee Holloway, Part II.

After ten minutes, when they finally realized I wasn't going to budge, they demanded all our money. We had four hundred pesos between us, and without hesitation, we forked it over. We triple power walked out of that alley with their words gringos estúpidos echoing in our heads. There's nothing like getting robbed at gunpoint by the local authorities.

Once we got to her hotel gate, she thanked me and gave me a kiss. When she was safely inside, I "shaked and baked" my way back to my hotel like I was avoiding the border patrol. It was like my name was Ramondo, and I was trying to get into Arizona.

I have not heard or seen from Elizabeth since. So, Elizabeth, if you've stumbled upon this book, what do you say we grab a bite to eat? If you're married or if your genetics have not been kind to you, a simple friend request on Facebook will suffice. I'm kidding. I don't care if you're now eligible to appear on *The Biggest Loser,* I'll still take you out for some dinner to reminisce about that night. Unfortunately, for my wallet's sake, we will have to cap your order off at two entrées. No grazing. I hope that's okay.

That week in Puerto Vallarta will always have a special place in my heart. It will probably always be my wildest and best vacation. I would go back there in a heartbeat. And I'd do it all the same, except I would probably avoid the beaches at night, and I'd also wear a biohazard suit to any foam parties. Gracias, Puerto Vallarta. Yo corazone tu.

THE DECISION

Picking where to go to college was a big decision. I eventually decided to leave the North Star State and take my talents to America's Dairyland I can't say for sure why. But what I do know is that I couldn't have chosen a better state to spend the next five and a half years of my life. Unknown to me when I made my decision, the state of Wisconsin really caters to my favorite activity—drinking. That's all there is to do there. Being a hardcore Minnesota Vikings fan, it's very hard for me to give any praise to the Cheesehead Nation. But I have to give credit where credit is due. Wisconsin is professional when it comes to drinking. It's like Germany mated with Ireland, and Wisconsin was the spawn. It stumbled out of the womb with a bottle of Jag in one hand and a brandy old fashioned in the other. What Wisconsin lacks in flashy nightclubs, ocean beaches, and densely concentrated population, it more than compensates for with its alcohol consumption. The concept is simple: any reason to crack a can of beer is acceptable. In the Badger State, all you do is combine an everyday activity with a case of beer.

It was not uncommon to get a phone call from a friend on a random Tuesday afternoon that went something like this: "Hey, the sun's out. Want to drink?" Or, "Oh my god! There's a couple of squirrels running around in my front yard! What do you say we get a case of beer and watch them from my porch?" I think there were even invites to bring over some mixers and watch my buddy's grass grow. I now take offense when people use the expression, "I'd rather watch grass grow," as if that's a negative. No, dipshit, you're just doing it wrong. Put a fifth of whiskey in your hand, and all of a sudden, watching a dandelion bloom turns your day into quite the hoot 'n' holler. Everyone in Wisco is down to have a good time, no matter what.

But don't think that you can just casually waltz into Wisconsin and start tossing 'em back like the local residents. It's like an elevation change. You have to get acclimated to it. The drinking in Wisconsin is parallel to the elevation of Mt. Everest. Countless visiting out-of-state friends dared to try the climb and become a true Wisconsin drinker. At the pinnacle of Everest one would find a little smiling badger with a platter of cheese and a pitcher of Leinenkugel's. Unfortunately for most of them, their trek to the summit ended before midnight, face down on the bar or passed out in a ditch. We lost a lot of good men. For the few that make it, their triumph doesn't last long. They usually fall off and hit every rock and ledge on the way down to a miserable Sunday morning hangover.

I can already see people from other states scoffing at my claims of Wisconsin being the mecca of drinking. There's probably some redneck down South who just knocked his spittoon all over his porch in outrage. Of course, he's listening to this via audiotape because he can't read. Five bucks says he just hit rewind to listen to the previous sentence. Now, he really has his overalls in a bundle. He shouts out to his cousin, "Hey, honey, this Yankee thanks he can out drank the great state of Ali-bamuh. General Lee is done rollin' in his grave right now. I challenge that sumbitch to cross that Dixie line. Roll, Tide."

Okay, easy, Cletus. Please don't exercise your right to bear arms. There's no doubt in my mind that you're the best at shotgunning a mason jar of your home-brewed moonshine. You can have that title, and the potential loss of vision that comes with every swig you take. But when it comes to nonfelony-sourced alcohol consumption, Wisconsin has that by a mile. Oh, and Cletus, one last thing, are your parents siblings?

I feel like Benedict Arnold talking up Wisconsin more than my home state of Minnesota. But it's true. Nationally, Minnesota is known for its "Minnesota nice" charm. Once again, I think Wisconsin has us beat. Go into any fast-food joint in Wisco, and you'll never see anyone more eager to serve you a Big Mac. The people are insanely friendly. I could leave my car parked in the middle of the street unlocked, with my windows down, keys on the front seat, and a winning Powerball ticket on the dash, and everything would still be there untouched the next morning.

Choosing to attend college in Wisconsin was the best choice of location I ever made. You have folks who are enormously friendly and like to drink anywhere, any-time. What more could anyone ask for? If you're walking down the street and see a group of strangers drinking and playing drinking games in the front yard, you're for sure going to get a cheer, and maybe even a free beer and an invitation to come play with them. The University of Wisconsin-Eau Claire was the specific college I chose to attend. There is not a better place that exemplifies these virtues, and it is my heaven on earth.

DISCLAIMER: By writing this chapter, I just broke the world record for bukkake by sucking off the entire state of Wisconsin. Let me reassure my fellow Minnesotans, I will never trade in my purple and gold for green and yellow, maroon and gold for red and white, or blue and red for blue and gold. So please, Minnesota, don't drown me in one of our pristine ten thousand lakes.

EAU CLAIRE COUNTY: THE REAL EAU C

The beautiful city of Eau Claire is nestled on the banks of the majestic Chippewa River an hour into Wisconsin from the Minnesota border. It's a smallish metropolitan area of sixty thousand peeps. Like my hometown, it's 120 percent white. Whenever I see a black person, I automatically assume the Packers are in town for a charity event. But aside from the occasional Donald Driver sighting at my grocery store, you won't find much else of note in Eau Claire.

It does not have any famous national landmarks. But it does have one of the cleanest and most bountiful groundwater reserves in the world. Although maybe that's not bragworthy because Mary Brunner was born and raised here, and she drank the very same water. You're thinking, who the fuck is Mary Brunner and why the fuck should I care? Does mass serial killer Charles Manson ring a bell? Little Mary was his girlfriend. So poke fun at the great city of Eau Claire if you want, but if so, I'm going to have to get all Helter Skelter on your ass.

The pulse of Eau Claire is the University. Not only does the university boast the city's tallest building at a whopping eight stories, it also serves as a symbol of glory that the entire community rallies behind—our mascot, the motherfucking Blugolds, bitch.

What the fuck is a Blugold, you ask? Did the town's founders mine gold, resulting in an industry-honoring name such as Tar Heels or Boilermakers? Or was there a local bird with sexy blue and gold feathers? No, all those logical answers are incorrect. We are named the Blugolds because the school colors are blue and gold. That's it. I wish I had been present at that meeting when the nickname was settled upon. I'm no historian but I have a pretty good idea of how it must have gone. "I got it! Our colors are blue and gold, right? BAM, Blugolds! We should hurry up and vote, two-for-one pitchers ends in ten minutes at the bar. All in favor say aye." Without hesitation, everyone yells aye. I have a notion that they were in such a hurry to get to the bar that they left out the "e" in the word "blue" when spelling Blugolds. Win.

I had no idea what to expect from UWEC on freshman move-in weekend. All I knew was that it was listed as a Tier 1 best Midwestern university (whatever that means), and was often referred to as the most beautiful campus in Wisconsin. So choke on that, Harvard.

I wasn't nervous about it. I had already squashed my biggest concern—that I would draw a random freak roommate—by deciding to room with one of my high school buddies, Bones. With my luck, a draw would leave me stuck with a gay gothic-boy who practices Wicca. The last thing I needed was to bring a chick back to my dorm room, only to interrupt a blood sacrifice to Lord Lucifer in the middle of the bedroom floor. Now that would be the cockblock of all cockblocks. So I am more than thankful I had secured a good buddy who was down with the three B's—bitches, blunts, and beer. (Yes, I'm well aware that phrase is really toolish.)

My mother did the mother thing and started crying during the move-in, partly because I was the first to leave the nest. But I think the main cause of the tears was that I am the favorite offspring. My father did the father thing and just wanted to get the fuck back to the air-conditioned truck after sherpa-ing my furniture up two flights of stairs.

Whatever. We said our good-byes, and Bones and I hit the futon to play some Xbox. Ten minutes later, the guy across the hall, Travis, came into our room and said, "I got four bottles of booze if you guys want to drink." YES. There's that Wisconsin charm I was talking about earlier.

We started kicking back some mixers and decided to skip all the freshman orientation bullshit. I'm sorry, but I don't need a seminar on the dangers of underage drinking. I think the "whiskey-seven" in my hand answered any concerns I may have had on that topic. All we needed was to get nice and sloppy for the freshman picnic that evening. You need a little bit of liquid courage when approaching a random female. I've tried it sober, but it's not very attractive when I can't even pronounce my one-syllable name. H-H-Hii, my name's J-J-J-AY.

When five o'clock rolled around, we had to meet up with our RA to head to the picnic. We mixed some drinks in twenty-ounce Sprite bottles for the road. The RA was like, "Wow, you guys are the most talkative freshmen I've ever had." Well, duh, Einstein. We were shit-bombed. The RA either didn't give a fuck or was a bit slow in the cranium. How else could he have missed the slurred speech, bloodshot eyes, and brown-tinted pop bottles?

When we arrived at the picnic, I was in heaven. I've never seen a higher concentration of beautiful girls in one area. (Of course, in the summer sun, every girl looks hot. It's not that the hotties hibernate in the winter; it's that any somewhat slim girl can throw on a pair of skimpy shorts and a pair of giant bug sunglasses. The girl looks hot until you go inside and the glasses come off, exposing her crossed eyes and blemished skin. This is just one more reason why I hate the sun. First, the sun started a lifelong battle against my pale skin. Racist. THEN, it decided to fuck up my climate. And now it's making my penis upset with what I put it in. Three strikes. Go fuck yourself, sun.)

I networked like crazy. The goal was simple: befriend as many girls as I could so that I could bring them to a house party as my admission ticket. That was easier than contracting AIDS in San Francisco. It's not that I wouldn't be allowed into a party without them; it's just disrespectful to do so. It's like being the guy showing up to a grill-out without any food or beer. You don't want to be a mooch. So, in order to gain the respect of the guys throwing the party, I gathered my stable of girls, and we left the picnic for my first college house party.

When we arrived, it was the usual routine. You pay your five bucks for a keg cup and watch a bunch of drunk girls dance around touching each other. To my surprise, there was an inflatable kiddie pool set up in the basement. Next to the pool, there were about ten industrial-size cans of chocolate pudding. It doesn't take a genius to figure out how the two items are related.

The owner of the house came down in a referee outfit. Am I an extra in *Old School*? You're my boy, Blue! He poured the cans of pudding into the pool, and within minutes, two girls came down in their bras and panties and jumped in. Boner. I got a front row seat to watch the gladiators fight to the bitter end—toplessness. Rip her bra off! After hundreds of body slams and bitchy hair pulls, my shirt was saturated in chocolate goo.

By the time I made it back to my dorm, I felt more beat up than the scissoring pudding beauties. My motor skills were gone. I fell over a four-foot retaining wall behind the dorm, landing peacefully in the sand-filled volleyball court. I woke up a few hours later with my head in a pile of puke and my mouth full of sand. So this is college? Perfect. I think I'm going to like this. The only thing that would have made that night better would have been waking up to a girl making a sandcastle around my wiener.

The next morning, Travis, Bones, and I were sitting in my dorm room hydrating with Gatorade when two guys rollerbladed in to greet us. They introduced themselves as Kach and Kyle. They too had skipped the freshman orientation to get hammered at a house party. Instantly, we became BFFs. Since all of our rooms were at the very end of our hallway, we decided to call our area the DX Corner. It was in dedication to the greatest wrestling posse of all time—Degeneration X. And if you're not down with that, I got two words for ya. SUCK IT.

OUT CHYA GET

How does one begin to describe one's first year of college? You have thousands of people your age living within five blocks of you. Half of the people living in your building are of the opposite sex. The campus provides everything you need on site. Compared to high school, college is the Walmart of partying. It makes everything you need for a successful party more accessible and efficient. For example:

Lodging

Let's say you somehow trick a girl into going back to your room for a game of one-on-one. In high school, you have to either buy a hotel room or sneak the girl into your house while your parents are sleeping. I would always get caught. My parents are light sleepers. My mom would bitch the next morning that her house is not my personal motel. I would counter with, "Yeah? Well, at least I'm not gay." That's when my dad would chuckle and take my side. That's always a dumb move in our house. If my mother is upset at us, we don't get dinner. And since neither my father nor I know what a kitchen is, we go hungry. In college, this situation is avoided because all you and the female have to do is take the elevator one floor up to your room. Efficient. With my own living quarters in college, I no longer had to worry about my tum-tum going empty.

Transportation

The biggest thing that sucked in high school was: if you're at a party you have no option but to drive home drunk. There's no way I was calling my mom at 3:00 a.m. to pick up my drunk ass. Plus, I used to think of drunk driving as a sport. I was like the UConn women's basketball team: undefeated. Don't judge me, MADD. Shit happens. Fortunately, in college everything was within walking distance, and I was able to retire from playing "keep it between the navigational lines." Again, efficient.

Hygiene

In high school, one of the most awkward moments was buying condoms. You'd be waiting to check out and your friend's mother would come in line behind you so you're forced to grab a tabloid magazine and nonchalantly slide it over the box. I just knew that nobody in the store believed I really cared about Angelina Jolie's latest Asian baby. Embarrassing.

College makes that embarrassment totally nonexistent. You can walk right up to the health center and receive a free sex-care package complete with condoms, lube, and an instructional pamphlet. Accessible. (I wish I still had that pamphlet. I always find myself doing the trampoline move when putting on a condom. All guys know what I'm talking about.)

Health Care

At this point in freshman year, college is alright. You can walk back from a party, bring a girl to your room, and have a full supply of condoms at your fingertips without a care in the world. Let's say you and the girl do the deed, but the condom breaks and your winky burns when you pee the next morning. No worries. College has you covered. As a matter of fact, you can both walk in together to get the morning-after pill and a free cotton swab test up your pee-hole right on campus. There's no more worry of having to go put Plan B on your parents' insurance bill like in high school. Again, accessible.

Side note: If you live in the Twin Cities area, don't buy the morning-after pill in the suburbs for forty bucks. Drive to the hospital in Minneapolis where you can get the pill subsidized. The only downside is that you have to wait in line with a bunch of cracked-out ghetto people who are talking too loud on their Bluetooths. But it's always entertaining to listen to a profanity-laced rant about something as simple as getting milk at the store: "Nah, mothafucka. You get tha mothafuckin milk at the sto. I'm gettin muh pills now. Quit playin, bitch. I love you, too. Bye."

Shopping List Completed, Party

Just like Walmart, your college campus is your one-stop shop. The DX Corner and I took advantage of all of these perks. (Except the cotton swab. Or at least that I'm aware of. Honestly, who would admit that?) With the time saved by the services provided by my campus, I was able to spend my time like a genuine patron of Walmart: being unemployed and drinking beer. 'Merica.

Well, you may ask, why wasn't your time spent studying? Because, idiot, freshman year you take all your lowest level general classes. Cakewalk. Being academically unchallenged, the DX Corner drank damn near every night. Why wouldn't you?

The only thing you have to worry about your first year is having your roommate come home early from class to catch you tugging your boat. Yeah, you'll get shit, but that only lasts until you catch him playing five-on-one. The best thing you can do is just fess up and admit it. Unless you have your pants at your ankles, sprawled out on the futon, drooling over a guy getting sandwiched by two horses on your big screen TV, you don't have to worry about any social repercussions. Every dude wanks it. Contrary to what your mother told you, you won't go blind. I'm proof of that. As for girls, I'm not familiar with what happens when you walk in on your roommate shoving a banana up her pudding void, but I assume it's the same thing. Who cares? Everyone does it. Even so, it's best to avoid getting caught rubbing one out by simply having sex with a real person. That's why freshman year is so great. Everyone wants to get laid. All the girls who were sheltered by their parents are ready to break out of their shackles. Blacks must have felt something like that when Lincoln signed the Emancipation Proclamation. Except that the blacks were excited to stop getting fucked in the ass, while the freshman girls were excited to get fucked in the ass.

The DX Corner had a very toolish saying related to the new sexual freedoms of the freshman girls: "Out-chya-get." That is simply the phrase you yell after having sex with a girl to get her out of your room. When the rest of us heard this yell, it was like a fire alarm. We would get out of our rooms to chant it down the hallway at the girl doing the walk of shame. Was it assholeish? Yes. Was it demeaning? Yes. Was it immature? Yes. Did we care? No. It was all in good fun. So if you're not down with out-chya-get, I want you to pull your head out your ass so you can hear me. I only have one thing to say to you: "OUT-CHYA-FUCKING-GET."

Unfortunately, the futon that my sweet little grandmother had so innocently given me in anticipation of an uplifting college experience became the bang-ton where the out-chya-gets occurred. All the members of the DX Corner had a ride on it. It was a disgusting, stinky slab of furniture by the end of the second semester. You'd be playing Xbox on it and turn your head to the side, only to find your face lying in a giant cumstain. It looked like it had been used as a barricade from a paintball arena. I bet I could have gotten enough cash for a semester of tuition if I had sold the cum-ton to a sperm bank. No doubt in my mind.

We did know that the only way to achieve cum-ton status was to pull a Soulja Boy and "supersoak that hoe." However, in telling the story, my homie Soulja Boy left out an important piece to the puzzle in "Crank That." You need alcohol. That's the only way you get action in college. In all honesty, that's the only way you can do anything in college. I've thought about going into detail about all the drunken dorm nights. But that's not really unique. Everyone does the same things in college.

You start your evening smooshed together on the futon with five dudes drinking beer, with a black light on, listening to pop radio. WHOOOO, party! Then the ladies show up (thank God). Your sudden relief at ending the sausagefest quickly turns sour as soon as the girls start talking about the total bitch down the hall in their dorm who hogs the hair dryer outlets in the bathroom. You pound more shots to drown out the cattiness.

Next, you all hoof it on icy sidewalks to a house party roughly a mile away. Along the way, you will have to stop your buddies from peeing on shit and talking smack to other guys walking by. The girls will be complaining the entire time about how cold they are, and how it sucks to walk in heels. You would like to punch them all in their faces because you can't understand how they haven't figured out in twenty years of living on this earth that wearing that shit in January is a dumb idea. But you don't because you know that kills all chances of getting laid, and you even offer them your jacket to wear in hopes that one of them will fall into your trap and return it at night's end to your room.

Once inside the party, you wait in line for what seems like an eternity to fill your keg cup. You are playing beer pong when all of the sudden the owners of the house herd everyone into the basement like cattle because the cops are there. The next three hours will be spent playing "Anne Frank" from the police. This sucks because everyone will start to piss all over the basement and you will be wading in urine. When the cops finally leave, you are free to exit the house and do the reverse hoof back to the dorms.

Once in the dorms, one of your crew guys will be roaming the hallways naked. Two other guys will be fighting, and maybe another guy is getting laid. The final guy will be shirtless trying to convince the RA that everyone has gone to bed while frantically trying to conceal the giant dick that someone drew on his chest with a Magic Marker while he was passed out.

You, on the other hand, will be sending a million texts to the girl who borrowed your jacket, trying to convince her to come to your room. The next morning you feel like an idiot going through your texts because she never responded to any of them. And for the cherry on the cake, you probably pissed your bed. I feel that's a pretty typical college night. So rather than beat a dead horse any further on things that every college kid already knows, I've assembled a five-step program for a successful freshman year.

THE FIVE STEPS TO A HEALTHY FRESHMAN YEAR

Step 1

My first step has to do with why you're in college in the first place. Academics. You know the old saying that two heads are better than one? Well, that's exactly what you need to learn in college.

I'm not telling you to cheat your way through college. But I am saying, pick your battles. Any course outside of your major is the battle to pick. I'm sorry, but if you're going to school for accounting, you are never going to be asked in an interview the atomic mass of boron. There's no need for an accounting major to spend hours in the library memorizing that bullshit periodic table. So how do you pass your classes? The first step is easy. Take general classes based on ease, not what interests you. Ratemyprofessor.com is a great resource to find out if a class is easy. If something interests you, use a thing called the Internet while you're hung over on Sunday to learn about it, not a class in school.

The next step is to take all your general classes with friends. That way you can share the workload. And among you and your friends, you will come up with someone who took the class a previous semester to get all the homework and quiz answers. Very rarely do professors change homework and quizzes in a 100-level class from semester to semester.

Last, in exams, sit next to your buddy. The professor is not going to see your eyes move in a fifty-thousand-square-foot lecture hall. If you are in an exam that allows graphing calculators, put all your notes and equations in a program. There's no way you should memorize all those calculus equations. You forget one letter in the equation, and the whole solution is fucked. I hate when I get the "Err" after I press Enter.

Cheating in your general classes is like speeding in your car on your way to work. Should you do it? No. But everyone does. Your major is like the workplace. You need to get there. And cheating is like speeding. Yes, I could leave twenty minutes earlier and get to my cubicle on time going the speed limit. But I want to finish watching two cousins making out on *Jerry Springer*. That extra time spent watching TV translates to not being in the library and going out to party. You only go to college once. Don't waste it going the speed limit in the library. Drive fast; take chances.

Step 2

The second step in my program is to not become buddies with your RA. I don't care how friendly he or she is when you first move in. You should be suspicious of anyone that friendly in the first place. Keep your friends close, and your enemies closer. Apologies to every gangster rapper who preaches that, but it's false. I want my enemy far away down the hall so he can't catch me riding dirty.

If you do become buddies with RAs, things get weird. They are going to want to hang out, and when you pull out a bottle of whiskey, it gets awkward. Do they look the other way, or do they write you up? Just avoid that scenario altogether. Find your crew and then distance yourself from every hallway activity. Eventually, they get the message and will stop knocking on your door to play flag football and other retarded bonding activities. Then you're free to do as you please in your room. We needed that freedom to drink. But that freedom could also be used to make a meth lab, marijuana dispensary, or makeshift whorehouse. The options are endless for any young, aspiring entrepreneur. The only time RAs will come knocking is if you're too loud. But even then, they don't have the authority to come into your room without permission. Just don't be dumb like me and open the door wide enough to expose all the alcohol bottles on your desk.

The only downside to alienating yourself is that you get blamed for every act of vandalism that takes place in the dorm. I remember one time someone shit in the urinal and the RA tried to blame me. I wish I had been the one who did it. So if your RA is a cocksucker, go into the bathroom at 4:00 a.m. and poke a dookie out in the urinal. Maybe put a flag in it that says, "Write me a drinking ticket again, bitch." That'll teach the motherfucker.

Step 3

The third step in the program is fairly obvious, but to some people it's not (me). You know those minitowers on campus that have the button to press if you're getting raped? Don't. Unless you're actually getting raped and not enjoying it. Press it then. Otherwise, it will cost you a hefty penny in the form of a "Disorderly Conduct-Misuse of an Emergency Phone Line" citation and an underage drinking ticket to boot.

In my defense, I was double dared. I had no choice. But that was a fun phone call to my mom the next morning. She did give me a great suggestion: the next time, I might as well walk right into the police station and shout, "I'm drunk and eighteen. Prosecute me as you please." I never did take that advice. But then again, I don't take much of my mother's advice.

Step 4

The last two steps in my program are a toss-up for importance. Here's the runner-up. It's not essential, but it makes college a whole lot easier: Get yourself a fake ID. Two reasons.

First, you don't have to rely on an older person to get you booze or, worse, tip them for the favor. The very worst thing is when you can't get ahold of your booze contact and you have to wait outside a liquor store and hit on strangers. They act as if you're trying to hire a hit man. It makes both parties uncomfortable, and you're highly likely to be stuck drinking Mountain Dew for the evening. Getting Dew-faced isn't quite the same as getting shitfaced.

Second, it will get you into the bars. House parties will get old. The true action in college is at the bars. I always had friends who had fakes and were too scared to use them at a bar. Dumb. The worst thing that can happen is that it gets taken away and you go home. You can't win the lottery if you don't buy a ticket.

If you're an Asian or a hot chick, acquiring a fake ID is easy. Asians all look the same to bouncers: you just have to match the date and sex. I've never seen an Asian bouncer, and Asians are the only ones who can tell each other apart. Do you really think a bar is going to hire a guy that is five feet tall and 120 pounds? Kung fu only works in the movies. An Asian bouncer is not going to stop a six-five, out-of-control drunk using some crouching tiger, hidden dragon bullshit.

If you're a hot chick, you only need to match your race. Hair color, eye color, and any other attributes are irrelevant. Ninety percent of people checking IDs at the door are male. Just make sure to push your boobs up and out. Even if you get the address wrong on the ID when they ask you, you're still getting in. If not, check to make sure there are no rainbow neon signs on the windows, or maybe it's time you call up Jenny Craig. For everyone else, life sucks. You better be prepared for the interrogation of a lifetime. You're going to need ten forms of second ID, and memorize every single detail on that fake. The best thing to do is invest in getting an ID made. Get one with your picture and name on it. You can do this online in a pinch. I was fortunate enough to get a call from a friend who knew an ID artiste. I had my mother transfer a hundred dollars into my account for an emergency purchase at the bookstore. Best decision I ever made.

Step 5

The final and most important step is not having a girlfriend freshman year. I made that horrible mistake twice because, frankly, I'm an idiot. College girls will drop you in a heartbeat if they think something is better. Usually, it's a bro who plays a sport for the school. Every girl thinks she will find the next Sidney Crosby. That just shows how dumb girls are. If you play the odds, that guy's future probably won't be going top shelf in the NHL. He's more likely to graduate with a degree in sociology (useless) and become a chronic alcoholic where his only reason to get up in the morning is to relive his glory days and beat his wife. After the fourth domestic violence call, the girl will finally realize she should have been slutting around the engineering department rather than the locker room.

For the record, I don't blame the athletes for getting the groupies. I'd do the same thing. Hate the game, not the player, homie. But still, I don't care how good of a guy you are, that's not going to stop your chick from getting stuffed by the fifth line defenseman. Take me, for example. I felt bad for just looking at the cleavage of another girl (for the record, 100 percent faithful), and what did that get me? It got me a steamy pile of shit on my face . . . twice.

Let me put it in perspective. Are you familiar with the six degrees of separation? If not, it's the theory that you will be connected to every person on the face of the planet within six person-to-person contacts. Thanks to my first girlfriend's promiscuous ways, my degree of separation is two. I am now Eskimo brothers with half the planet. (Just so you know, as I'm writing this, I'm air-fiving all the guys reading this to our newfound brotherhood.) Ironically, I am not mad at her at all. She came to me and was honest about her labia's addiction to penis. I hold nothing against her.

My second girlfriend, however, will deny her addiction to the day she dies. I can't stand liars. Any excuse or justification that comes out of her mouth for "falling" on those dicks is hodgepodge. She will lay down for any guy like France did for Germany in World War II. I don't care if she's getting waterboarded while bamboo slivers are being shoved up her fingernails, she will not tell the truth about her whorish behavior. Due to her treachery, I woke up every morning hoping that she would become the middle piece in the human centipede. For those of you who think that's taking it too far, you are sorely mistaken. The way I see it, she was feeding me shit out of her mouth, so why not return the favor? An eye for an eye, motherfucker.

Cheating bitches aside, fellas, you still don't want a girlfriend freshman year. Why lock into something in the prime of your youth when you don't know what the outcome will be? Sure, she may be the hottest thing on campus, but let me tell you, college is a gauntlet on the body. When her high school metabolism poops out, and the Four Loco binges combined with the cafeteria food catch up to her, she's going to look like an air pump was hooked up to her ass. Sir Mix A Lot can have that. My anaconda don't want none if you got buns, hun.

I suppose you could make the argument that heftier girls give better blowjobs. But even then, you have to batter up your dick and deep fry it like a corndog for her to want it. No thanks, that grease is fucking hot. All I'm saying is that you don't want to be stuck with a girl who transforms into Optimus Prime in only two years.

And please, don't give me the bullshit that she's pretty on the inside and really smart. I've never heard a guy say, "DAAAAAAMMNN. I want to go balls deep in that girl's brain." For starters, that would kill her. You're looking at eighteen to life for that.

Second, the inside beauty excuse is just something that ugly women who can't get laid and turn feminist say. What those feminists need to do is stop focusing so much energy on hating the penis and handcuff their fat ass to a treadmill. At the very least, they could change their diet to strictly Slim Fast and ex-lax. So don't listen to them. Do you really want to take advice from a woman who has a military haircut and refuses to shave her body hair? I didn't think so. Case closed.

After my fat chick rant, I suspect that I will be receiving an adoring phone call from Michelle Obama to become her lead spokesman in her campaign against obesity in America. We are essentially saying the same thing. NO FAT CHICKS. I will, of course, accept her offer.

So, incoming freshman guys, I think I speak for both Michelle and myself when I say, wait on having a girlfriend in college. Bang as many chicks as you can while they're still hot. After your junior year, scope the field out. If a girl still looks good after three years of college, she's probably a keeper. Trust me, you'll be much happier this way. Don't be kicking yourself down the road like I am for wasting your freshman year on girlfriends.

Conclusion

So there you have it. Your blueprint for success. It's up to you to execute it. If you follow these five simple steps, it will be the best year of your life. If not, I will wait in the bushes at your house in a year from now so I can jump out and say, "I told ya so, bitch." Trust me. You don't want that. I can be very annoying and sometimes creepy. Your neighbors will call 911 about the crazy man loitering in your bushes. Save yourself the humiliation and follow every word I have written.

DETOX SO I CAN RETOX

A lot of my friends headed straight for private universities Not me—too many red flags. Most private schools segregate dorms by gender, enforce zero-tolerance alcohol policies, and forbid the opposite sex in your dorm room past 10:00 p.m. In my case, that would be like jumping into shark-infested waters with bacon wrapped around my dick. Public university all the way. I'm really glad I based my future on whether or not I could have a female in my dorm room past ten. Intelligent.

Picking a college is like selecting a player in the NFL draft. The only difference is that I was making my selection based on non-high character values. I was looking for a Randy Moss over a Tim Tebow. Do I attend a college where I play when I want to play, spray water bottles at authority figures, and smoke weed every blue moon? Or do I stay a virgin, read the Bible, and never see any action on the field? I'm picking the straight cash homie all day long.

Every private school has behavior policies that Tim Tebow would get a boner over. That's why I didn't attend one. However, I need to make an important distinction when it comes to private schools, so I don't lump them all into one stereotype. There are two types of private schools:

1. The private school where you need to be smart and rich to be admitted.
2. The private school where you just need to be rich.

The first type would be my hellhole. No parties and all ugly girls. What can be worse than that? Nothing. I know this because I have a female cousin the same age as me who landed a full ride to one of these schools. Normally, having a female cousin at a different university is a direct pipeline to a whole new plethora of girls that you can tap into. Drill, baby, drill. Unfortunately, you will find no refined oil coming from this pipeline, only crude. Every Thanksgiving, my smart female cousin would bring photo albums featuring all the great community charity events she and her friends engaged in on the weekends for "fun." Not one photo had a beer in it, and all the girls looked like Ugly Betty. Puke. Not worth my time to even ask her if I could visit her school for a weekend. For me to pass up a whole pipeline of girls, you know it's bad. You'd probably have more fun and find a better looking GGILF (great grandmother I'd like to fuck) at a retirement home. At least there, you could steal some prescription pills and get a GJ. A GJ is a gum job. I think that's self-explanatory.

The second kind, where you just have to be rich, is great. That kind is where all my friends who chose private schools went. They party. It worked out great for me because I got to visit them on the weekends and was immune from their university's moral rules, while still getting to reap the benefits, number one of which was the girls.

It's not that private school girls are necessarily more attractive than public school girls, but coming from wealthier families, they have the disposable income to "put their face on" 24/7. They don't have to ration their beauty supplies. You never see a private school girl without her hair and makeup done. Whether she's jogging, pooping, or going to the bar, she always looks good. Especially when she's pooping. So hot.

I think their 24/7 hotness is great because I hate getting tricked. If you meet a private school girl at a bar, she will always look as advertised. She will be up an hour earlier than you getting ready, and when you wake up, she will still look gorgeous like the night before at the bar. Public school girls, not so much. You may see the girl on campus the next day in sweatpants and think, what the fuck happened, who did this to you?

The public school girls are like a fast food commercial. The food looks really good when you see it on TV, but when you go to order it the next day, it looks like it was cooked three days prior and reheated in a microwave. Some girls should be sued for false advertising.

A less obvious and nonphysical benefit to private school girls is the trust fund nest eggs they have waiting for them. If you happen to knock one up, it's less of a burden on you than if you knocked up a trailer park queen. You don't have to worry about child support. The private school girl will either pay for the abortion or keep the zygote, and you get to suck off the teat of her parents' wallet for the rest of your life. Win/win. I wouldn't even bother bringing condoms to visit a private school.

The only contraceptive that will get in your way of making the American dream come true and becoming a stay-at-home daddy for the rest of your life is the private school guys. Not all, but a good number of them, have shades of the frat guy attitude, which means they think they are awesome for no apparent reason. The shades of frat boy you find in a private school guy are like a watered-down black person. Think Alicia Keys. She has some cream diluting her coffee.

I hate frat boys. The whole concept of an eternal brotherhood is gay. The only reason you join a frat is because you are either too unathletic to make a sports team, or you're too socially awkward to make your own friends. Why else would someone tolerate borderline gay initiations and be a bitch to a house full of guys for your first year of college? "Thank you, sir, but I don't want another." The only benefit of joining a frat is if you're a drug dealer or rapist and would like to get your hands on every fraternity's endless supply of roofies and chloroform There is absolutely no other excuse. The best example I can give to demonstrate the frat-boy side of a private school dude is when I went to visit my high school friends at St. John's University my sophomore year of college.

St. John's is a small college located an hour and a half northwest of Minneapolis. I went to visit my friends on freshman move-in weekend. That is the best weekend of the school year at any college. I have every school in a hundred-mile radius of my home circled on my calendar for that special time. Even if you are a fifth-year supersenior, I strongly suggest you attend the picnics and activities.

It's like an auto convention. It's your first chance to scope out the latest models for the current year. Maybe if you're lucky, you get to test drive a few and see how they handle. Personally, I will never forget the 2007 models. That was a good year. The cars that year were very user friendly and easy to drive. They just don't make 'em like they used to. (Or the more plausible explanation is just that I'm four years older now and that much creepier when I attend the auto convention.)

Anyway, as I was visiting my buddies at the private school, we were trying to get the freshman girls to come to a house party. I think we failed. I can't really remember. But the most likely scenario is we failed, so I will go with that. What I do remember is getting my first taste of the fratty private school guy. You know you are at a private school party when the first thing someone says to you as you walk through the door is, "Who do you know here?"

Fuck you, guy. That's the biggest douchebag question in the world. That's not an honest inquiry. It's a smartass way of asking, "Who the fuck are you, and why are you at my house?" I always throw out a common white guy name like Mike or Ben and say I went to high school with them. It works every time. There's always a Mike at every party. It's quite a shame that one has to resort to trickery and tomfoolery to get into a party. When you walk through the door of a party at a public university, you're given a red Solo cup and directions to the keg. No questions asked. That's what I'm talking about.

Once inside a private school party, the frat boy attitudes just keep coming. They get overzealous about common party activities. For example, let's say one of them bongs a single beer. He will be rewarded with high fives and self-proclaim that he is totally awesome. To me, that would be like Terrell Owens taking out the Sharpie for catching a three yard out on first down. Give me a break. Act like you've been there. You only bust out the Sharpie if you take a weed hit, hold the smoke, bong the beer, take a shot, and then blow the smoke out in someone's face while you're taking a piss outside. Or, in football terms, you caught a TD pass in triple coverage, one handed, on a broken leg.

The toolish fratty behavior of a private school guy is just something you have to put up with. They're like gnats. Yes, they are an annoyance, but it doesn't bother you enough to leave. You tolerate them in hopes of landing one of the gorgeous girls who attend their pow-wows.

Easier said than done.

A guy can take getting turned down only so many times before he calls it a career and retires. That night I definitely tried to stretch my career, much like a washed-up player who should have retired many years ago. (I'm talking about you, Favre.) With my career finally coming to an embarrassing end, we decided to head back to the dorms. Little did I know that the night would soon become a little bit livelier.

Meandering across campus to my friend's dorm, I noticed a loading dock. It intrigued my drunken brain. I got on the dock and began throwing crates off it. Wise. What is it about destroying things when you're drunk? You just can't help yourself. The same can be said for smelling your own farts. You know the outcome is going to be unpleasant, but you do it anyway.

Let's just say that campus security was not amused by my antics. Rather than yield to them, I took off running. Let the chase begin. Being chased is fun. I was giggling the whole time, yelling "fuck you" in a high-pitched girly voice every time they told me to stop. I had no idea of the layout of the campus. I picked a direction, and I just started runn-ang. You can insert the generic, "Run, Forrest! Run!" here. I have fairly decent land speed for a nonKenyan, so when I finally believed I had lost the security guards, I decided to hide under a pine tree. Unfortunately for me, the pine tree was a sapling and might as well have been a palm with leaves beginning fifty feet up. Absolutely no foliage was concealing me from my pursuers.

I heard a guard yell, "Don't move. I will taze you." My inebriated brain was baffled. How could the guy see me? Does he have x-ray vision? Fearing a couple thousand volts of electricity flowing through my veins, I threw in the towel. I was a fugitive no more. They handcuffed me and called the "real" police to the scene. Since I wasn't a student of this university, the security guards kicked me off the campus, and the police, having nowhere else to bring me, decided to take me to the Stearns County Detox Center.

Detox is an entertaining experience. I think it's worth a trip. However, I wouldn't make a habit out of it. It's like visiting a national monument. Oh, look, there's Mt. Rushmore. Fascinating. But would I ever want to go see it again? Fuck, no.

My detox experience began at 3:30 a.m. when I was handed a standard-issue blue jumpsuit and escorted to my cell. I immediately snuggled under the scratchy covers, making sure to sleep on my back for fear of any unwanted butt-play by my roommate. I woke up in the morning and surveyed my new home.

I figured the residents of the detox facility would be comprised of mainly dumb, drunk college kids—like me. Nope. It was like an insane asylum. When I opened my eyes, my fifty-year-old cellmate was sitting on his bed and staring at me. I have no idea how long he had been doing that. All I know is that my poop-trap still felt tight and unviolated. I introduced myself and told my story of how I ended up there.

He didn't say anything back. Feeling awkward, I resorted to every prison movie I'd ever seen and asked, "What are you in here for?" What else are you supposed to say? He smiled and said he'd been in there for five days coming down from a meth and LSD-induced bender. Wonderful.

He brought me out to the main lounge where all the inmates congregate. For him, it was like a class reunion. He knew everyone. I was introduced to the whole gang. There was his female friend who couldn't stop convulsing in the corner. She was nice. He had another buddy who didn't respond to anything, just stared blankly at the wall as if he had just had a lobotomy. But my personal favorite was the guy who paced up and down talking to himself. He was a real winner. If MTV was smart, they would cast these people into the *Real World* house. At least the title would be accurate.

The nurses noticed that I was up and came over to explain my situation to me. By law, I was required to stay at detox for twelve hours—until 3:30 p.m. Of course, with my luck, I had not driven to St. John's, and my ride home had already left at 9:00 a.m. to get to work. So, as usual, my mother received a great phone call. She was really happy. She loves dropping all of her afternoon and evening plans and driving an hour and a half to pick up her twenty-year-old son from detox. She's so proud of me.

I spent the day being entertained by all the crazies. When medication time came, it was like throwing feed at the petting zoo. They all stampeded the medicine cart. Think Black Friday. After one guy got his meds, he was able to leave detox and be released back into the wild. He immediately changed into his street clothes—a DARE shirt. Am I the only one that finds humor in that?

When 3:30 p.m. finally rolled around, I changed into my clothes and collected my personal belongings. I got into my mother's car, and let's just say, I've had better road trips. There was really nothing to say. Her stern verbal beating made me feel about as much self-love as a twenty-dollar hooker who's getting drilled by anyone to pay for baby formula.

I did learn a few useful things. A night in detox costs roughly $350—about as much as a one-night stay in a high-class hotel. Sure, the amenities aren't quite as nice, but for sheer entertainment value, it's worth it. You're only going to find a better show in Vegas. The best part of this show is that it is possible to say, "Fuck the $350." Here's the secret that the people at detox don't want you to know. Call them, tell them you're a full-time student and don't have a job, and thus you can't pay your bill. Charges dropped. No questions asked. Perfect.

What else did I learn that particular weekend? This: No matter which area code I'm in, I will strike out with girls, and because of it, I will end up doing dumb things like throwing crates off a loading dock, which will lead to negative consequences. If I had gone "two in the pink, one in the stink" like I should have, instead of crate throwing, detox would have never happened. So ladies, next time you selfishly turn me down, think about what will happen to me later that night. Do you want that on your conscience for the rest of your life? I didn't think so. So let's make whoopie.

THE PHYSICS OF COLLEGE

I use the word physics in the title of this chapter because that is one subject I can't wrap my brain around. How the tennis ball and bowling ball hit the ground at the same time blows my mind. I just don't get it. Another thing I don't get is all the crazy people on a college campus. There's always some group that sets up a table on campus and sits around all day trying to "enlighten" me. Why the fuck do I care about what some knobjob thinks?

College should be a place where people from different backgrounds and viewpoints can share ideas and agree to disagree. But often times if you disagree with the crazies, you're looked at like you're a serial child rapist who should be castrated and thrown into the depths of hell (which all chi-mos should be). I'm glad you've found something you're passionate about, but don't get mad at me if I don't share the same passion for saving the fucking manatee when I live in the middle of the goddamn country. The closest I've been to a manatee is the girl who slept in my bed last night. So lay off.

All throughout college, crazy people are going to try and get you to join a cause or protest. What's the fucking point? I never joined any stupid club or organization on campus my entire five years. Why would I waste my time holding a sign all day trying to convince people to think like me? If that's how you want to spend your day, that's fine, but I have a twelve-pack in the fridge that needs tending to.

The worst group to not show support for on every campus is the gay-lesbian-bisexual-transgender organization (GLBTG). That was the old acronym. By now, they probably added on some new letters to include all the other weird sexual orientations. If you don't have a rainbow flag in your hand, you are apparently a homophobe and should be exiled. No. I just don't give a shit that you fart out glitter. Your anus has a higher threshold of pain than mine. Big fucking deal. Why do you get to throw big flamboyant festivals on campus for that achievement? I can stand on one foot for an extended period of time. Where's my parade?

If you're gay and want to pinch your boyfriend's butt in public, go for it. I won't judge. As long as I can't feel the heat from you gazing at my ass like a laser beam, I'm okay with whatever else you do. What a man puts up his own ass in the comfort of his own home is his choice. This is America. Nowhere in the Constitution does it say that you can't tear up your sphincter. As long as you have health insurance and I don't have to pick up the tab for your stitches, have at it. The only thing I'm against is using hamsters. That's animal cruelty. Poor Lemmiwinks.

As annoying as the GLBTG organization can be, it isn't the only group that annoys the hell out of me. The second worst type of group on campus is the ultra-religious crazies. Every fall semester these insane preachers from down South come on campus and lecture all the students walking by on their way to class. They come from those churches that speak in tongues. What is up with that shit? By placing their hand on someone's forehead and blabbering off gibberish, they can heal people? Whatever drug they're on, I want some. I've heard of getting high on faith, but that looks more like an acid trip.

I would skip class all day long to be entertained by these loonies. Their message was that basically every single person except them was going to hell. All activities were for the devil except eating, sleeping, and breathing. One of the preachers told me I was going to hell because I had an AC/DC shirt on, and rock and roll music is for the devil. Wow. I was thunderstruck. I found that odd, considering that Jesus looks like he could easily fill in for any hard rock band.

Don't think that it's only the social groups on campus that try to turn you crazy. Some of the professors are even worse. It gets really annoying when you just want to learn about rocks in geology class without having to hear shit about politics. What does magma have to do with George Bush? Then again, we did light up Saddam's ass like Popocatepetl. So, in that regard, I guess they're kind of related.

To understand why professors preach this shit, it's important to understand where a majority of them came from. They are campus lifers. They got their bachelor's and then eventually their PhD. Then the university hired them. They never left. How a university operates is the extent of their world-view. That is a horrible model to mold the world after. They think that everyone can just sit on the campus mall all day, barefoot, listening to Phish and throwing a Frisbee around to each other in perfect harmony. Yeah, you go to Pakistan and have fun trying to do that. You'll toss them a Frisbee and get a pipe bomb thrown back in return.

Some of the things I've heard come out of these professors' mouths are ridiculous. They want you to be just like them. My professor drives an electric car, so I should too. How about no. Unless you have a solar panel roof and a wind turbine in your front yard, where do you think your electricity to power your car comes from? Magic? No, it comes from a goddamn coal plant. All you're doing is trading one environment-polluting fossil fuel for another. Check yourself before you wreck yourself, fool. Until someone invents a hydrogen-powered car (zero fossil fuel), I'm not drinking the hybrid Kool-Aid from my hippie teacher.

In my very first college course, I had a crazy professor. She lectured us on using politically correct language. (If you haven't noticed, I didn't pay attention.) She went on a rant about how it's not businessman, it's businessperson, and blah blah blah. The icing on the cake was when she wanted to start a movement to change the spelling of "woman" to "womyn." The reasoning was to eliminate the "man" part because it's degrading.

ARE YOU FUCKING KIDDING ME? However, I got the last laugh when I would ask questions throughout the semester to get her to come to my computer. She thought I was confused on the material, but in reality, I just wanted her to rub her big feminist tits on my shoulder. They were huge. Got ya', bitch.

I got corrected in another class when we were reading a book and I raised my hand to answer a question about the fat kid in the book. As soon as fat kid left my mouth, the instructor cut off my verbal misdemeanor and said I should use weight challenged instead. Seriously? If we want to get politically correct, there's a ton of other words I could have chosen. Like nutritionally incompetent or fitness deficient.

I was thankful that I chose to become a business major and didn't have to hear all that hellishly annoying bullshit once I got done with my general classes. At least in the business school, you can still say "God Bless" or "Merry Christmas." If I had uttered those phrases outside the business building, I would have been looked at like the second coming of Hitler. I have no problem with Jews, I swear. Jesus was a Jew, and he's my homeboy.

Uh-oh. I slipped up in the previous paragraph and revealed my true identity. I am a business major, ergo, I must value only money and getting rich, no matter how many people I squash in my way. STOP, PUT THE TORCH AND PITCHFORK DOWN, AND HEAR ME OUT. In this country, everyone is entitled to a fair trial. Let me defend myself. I shouldn't have to, but in college, you're treated like a leper with AIDS if you value capitalism.

The basis of my defense is the principle of stare decisis, or in layman's terms, a precedent established by prior situations or decisions. The earliest historical situation that can help bolster my defense is how society was structured by our nation's earliest inhabitants, the Indians (feather, not dot). You see, before we essentially stole all the Indians' land for three pots, a fork, and smallpox, we observed how their society worked. Every morning, all the braves went out to hunt and bring back buffalo for the tribe to eat. There was one brave named Tonto who, in particular, was "cash money" when it came to slaying the delicious bison. He more than gladly gave his share to the tribal elders and the disabled Indians who were off making clay sculptures out of the buffalo pies. It's only right to provide for those who can't provide for themselves.

As time continued, the other braves began to get frustrated with their inability to bring back as much meat as Tonto. One by one, they began to say, fuck it, Tonto's got my appetite covered. So what did these braves do? They decided to stop hunting and hung out in their wigwams puffing the peace pipe all day and pooping out more babies with their squaws. Now, Tonto had to bring back more buffalo to feed all the bastard babies.

Tonto was busting his ass to bring the buffalo back. When he had to start giving more and more meat to the tribe, he began to think, fuck this shit. Why should I feed Lazy Horse while he puff-puff-passes all day? One morning he packed up his teepee and headed out to find a new tribe. What became of the tribe he left behind? They died. All of them. The cause of death was starvation. THE END.

That story is 100 percent historically accurate. Don't even bother Wikipedia-ing it. Take my word. The moral of the story is that a good member of society will give help to those who need it. But when people start abusing that good faith, and ask for more until they are dependent on it, eventually the Tontos will pack up their shit and leave. At that point, our society would collapse and turn into post-Cold War Russia. Gross. I hate vodka.

Am I right or wrong on capitalism? That's for the judge in this completely made-up trial to decide. But at least I've made my case, and it makes sense in my mind. It's like having that friend who lives on your couch for five months without paying rent. Eventually, you're going to give him the ultimatum of find a job or get the fuck out.

So where does this all leave me? Obviously, I have demonstrated that I don't see eye to eye with many of the entities trying to influence me on my college campus. I know it ruffles their feathers, seeing that they were unsuccessful in molding me into the socialist, atheist, hybrid-driving, politically correct wiener that is the final product they export into the real world. Not sorry about it. But at the same time, I give kudos to their effort. They are resilient, no doubt about it.

For the longest time, I was able to ignore their efforts because I simply didn't give a shit. However, that all changed when the crazies decided to infiltrate my personal life and wage war. They decided to attack my home. My home is the street in my college town where all my favorite bars are. I live there. They attacked my place of residence by initiating smear campaigns on campus attempting to deter people from going to the bars. They essentially claimed that the bars force people to get drunk and are full of racist, sexual predators capitalizing on that circumstance.

To me, this was a direct slap to the very fabric I am made of and, thus, a declaration of war. Their false rumors persuaded incoming freshmen to be wary of going to the bars and, in some cases, halted them from attending altogether.

It's like in the Civil War when the Union Army blew up all the railways that provided supplies to the Confederate Army. Without a fresh supply of freshman girls for me to creep out, going to the bar would be a lost cause. Well, I'm not going to allow that. I will defend my home like Mel Gibson in *Braveheart*. "They will never take OUR FRESHMEN!"

Let me go on the defensive and put the rumors to rest regarding my homeland. I have never seen any bartender get on horseback and go around town lassoing people, dragging them into a bar. Nor does the door lock behind you once you enter the bars. And finally, I have never been ambushed inside a bar with a syringe full of vodka by any employee. Every retarded thing you engage in is your choice. It's ridiculous to blame anyone but yourself if you get too drunk and decide to start humping a cop car in the parking lot The bar did not make you put your wiener in the gas tank.

And furthermore, just because the demographics of the bars comprise mainly Caucasians, that does not mean the bar is racist. Ninety percent of the music played by the DJs is from black artists. I've never been to a Ku Klux Klan rally, but I can't imagine the Imperial Wizard is teaching everyone how to Dougie in front of the burning cross. ALL MY WHITIES LOVE ME. ALL MY, ALL MY, WHITIES LOVE ME. YOU CAN'T FUCK WITH MY DOUGIE. No. That doesn't happen. The notion of these bars breeding hate is ridiculous. The only things these bars breed are unplanned pregnancies.

If the crazies don't want to get hammered at a bar, that's fine. I don't care. But don't tread on me and my love of being plastered. I don't see you convincing me otherwise, so quit the smear campaigns on excessive drinking at the bar. I need that new crop of freshmen to show up every year. If you agree to that, I will tolerate the crazy professors, politically correct lingo, and dipshit social groups on campus. You see, kids, that's called a compromise.

Going forward, I promise this is the only time I'm going to bring up heavy shit in the book. Well, except for my chapter on abortion. KIDDING. No such chapter. I could care less if a girl wants to stick a coat hanger up there and scramble that fetus. That way, my tax dollars don't have to pay for her nugget later on, when she can't afford it. I also feel that's a better option than her going Casey Anthony on the kid. Ladies, you'd have a better shot at winning the lottery than receiving the verdict she got. So keep that in mind.

829 CHIPPEWA

829 Chippewa is the address of my first college house. Everyone has love for their first college house. It's the same kind of love you have for a red-headed stepchild. You show your love by beating the shit out of it. I signed the lease to this house with the rest of the DX Corner. If that house was a child, we would all be serving consecutive life sentences for child abuse, neglect, and possibly rape. Kudos to the builder of that house. Because it survived us I'd feel comfortable bunkering down in it during a nuclear holocaust.

The number one lesson to learn with your college house: Have a spare room because people are going to fuck at your parties. And this is just personal preference, but I'd much rather have a designated "fuck room" than have people use my bedroom. I'm not too keen on finding a tumbleweed of random pubes blowing through my sheets, or some dried uterine lining staining my mattress. Unless you're some pervert and like sleeping on random human secretions, the spare room is a necessity. (Side note on the topic of banging chicks on the flow: you can wade in the red river, just don't drink from it.)

Our spare room looked like a human trafficker had been the interior designer. The only piece of furniture was an old futon mattress. Unfortunately, that meant the room had to double as a biowaste and latex garbage dump. I never ventured in there. I didn't need to inhale syphilis spores into my lungs.

One night in particular that room saw a lot of ass. It was the night we threw our first house party to break in the new school year. Normally, I am not a fan of themed parties because they're flat-out gay. But if you can have a theme that overpowers the gayness, then I'm okay with it. Bones, Kach, Kyle, and I decided that a fine theme for our first party would be Playboy. The dress code was simple: girls wear lingerie and guys wear their normal street clothes. It was perfect. Win/win for every guy in attendance. You get to see girls in strings and napkins without ever having to see a hairy nutsack slip out of the banana hammock. The female figure is way more attractive. Why taint the night's beauty with frontal male nudity?

In preparation, I enlisted the help of my father. From what I understand, most father/son bonding time is accomplished through fishing. Like any guy, I love fishing. But to catch the species of fish I was going after, I needed a special kind of pole. I was trying to wrangle the elusive pink-gilled tuna, and so that would be, of course, a stripper pole. My father and I fabricated a wonderful piece of equipment, which I brought back and set up in the basement of my new house. It may not have been the *Field of Dreams*, but if you build it, they will come. (In this case, that phrase can be taken literally.)

The Playboy party went off swimmingly. Mid-party, after refilling my keg cup, I took a moment to scan the room. Half-naked, beautiful women dancing around, my buddies playing beer pong, and everyone having a good time! How could this be anything but the America Jefferson envisioned for us in the Declaration of Independence? Life, Liberty, and the Pursuit of Happiness is code for Beer, Party, and Stripper Poles.

The part they don't teach you about in history class is the party that the Patriots threw after Cornwallis bent over and surrendered. I feel certain it was nearly identical to this one. Madison and Washington owned the beer pong table all night, Franklin's fat ass was passed out on the couch, Jefferson brought a bag of his freshly harvested marijuana, Martha Washington was getting freaky on the stripper pole, and Paul Revere rode home drunk on his horse. The main difference is that the Founding Fathers probably had slaves to wait in line for them to get their keg cup refills. I've had to wait minutes on end in the keg line, and it's torture.

If you walked into our house at 829 Chippewa after any one of our parties, you would think you were in Hiroshima, circa 1945. All our doors were kicked in, windows broken, furniture destroyed, and there were beer streaks running down the walls. When our lease was up, we didn't clean a damn thing. When you have a party house, the damage deposit is like a black father—it ain't coming back. You won't win. I learned that lesson watching the guys in the boiler room of the *Titanic* trying to beat the Atlantic Ocean. Fuck that. I'd probably be the dumbass that jumps overboard and bounces off the propeller. That's actually the best part of the entire film.

And don't feel bad for the landlords. You can clean the whole place up spotless, and they are still going to find some way to hold on to your damage deposit. So trash that fucking house. Go big or go home. It's not like college houses are maintained to a high standard by the landlord anyway. The only way a college landlord is going to repair anything is if he is one warning away from the city nailing up a Condemned sign.

Landlords don't do shit for you. One winter evening our furnace went out. It just happened to be twenty degrees below zero. The cheapass gave us three space heaters to heat a house of six guys for the next three days. I looked like the Michelin Man when I went to bed, and I woke up with icicles in my nose. It was horrible. Do you know how desperate I had to be to sleep in the library instead of my own home? That's like when the kids jumped into the outhouses in *Schindler's List*. It's a shitty option, (no pun intended), but it's better than dying.

So throw as many parties as you can. You don't throw parties because you like living in a shithole that smells like a hamster cage. You throw parties to attract girls. Every male species in the animal kingdom does something to attract the opposite sex. Turkeys puff up their feathers, deer grow antlers, and dueling flatworms simply try to spear the female with their penis (seriously, look it up). Some human males play sports. Some guys juice it up. Some guys buy expensive cars. Other guys are blessed with a giant ding-a-ling and intentionally leave the door open every time they take a piss. I don't have any of those methods of attraction. Therefore, I throw parties.

The crazier the parties you throw, the stronger your pheromones will be. Do not be afraid to be a rock star. Let your house be as badass as a Mötley Crüe hotel room. The best activities are those traditionally intended for outside use only: supersoakers, bicycles, and backyard wrestling. Combine those with traditional indoor party activities: kegs, club lights, stripper poles, and loud music. Stir well to create an atmosphere of anarchy. I promise you that it will rub off on the girls, and you will be occupying their pants like Wall Street.

Don't get upset about anything your guests do. If a guy wants to be Tarzan on your chandelier, let him. Duct tape can fix that. If a guy mistakes the living room for the bathroom, that's okay. Throw newspaper over it. If someone wants to make a Slip 'n Slide on your wood floors with cooking oil, let them. Who gives a shit?

I will say that it's better to be present when your guests do these sorts of things. My roommates and I had a tendency to abandon our guests and slip out to a bar. It would have been better to at least have known about the fun times with the cooking oil. The next morning it was really pathetic to be one of five college-educated guys totally stumped as to why all the beer on the floor hadn't evaporated yet. When we found the empty Crisco bottle, we felt like Gilbert Grape.

We were generous and loving neighbors, and left our house open at all times. This was a great idea—until the pranks started. The worst one was when someone took all the labels off our canned foods. You'd come home starving with your fingers crossed for chicken noodle soup, only to find goddamned creamed corn. I secretly suspect that my mother did it, so I would eat my vegetables. Not cool, Mom.

Was the mayhem and debauchery worth it? Absolutely! I get teary eyed just thinking about dear old 829 Chippewa. Never in your life are you going to be able to behave in an out-of-control manner like you do in your first college house. Don't take that for granted. My former roommates and I simply called it the Promised Land. I think that explains it. I urge you to make your own Promised Land. Don't worry about any of the negative consequences from doing so. When you look back, all those consequences will be well worth it.

METH HEALS YOU

My biggest regret for my college years is not staying in my college town during the summer. I could have hung out with my friends drinking beer in a yard all day or floated down the river on a tube. But, every summer I crossed back over the border to Minnesota to a forty-hour-a-week blue-collar job for a construction company, pouring concrete in residential areas.

At the time, I was unable to appreciate the beauties of waking up at 5:00 a.m. and driving across town to do manual labor in the sun for eight hours. But now that I have worked a desk job in the white-collar world, I miss many of the precious little things in life that were available only at the construction site. Isn't that what life is all about? The little things? Things like being able to cough, scratch my nuts, burp, swear, and fart at my leisure. You can try and let one rip in the office, but that building is quieter than a deaf classroom. The girl in the cube next to me queefs loud and clear at least once a day. Gross.

If you are able to silence one out, someone will always walk into your cube ten seconds later. You know that if you can smell it, they can, too. But you both have to play it off like your ass fumes aren't present. God, is that awkward trying to have a normal conversation when your nostrils are tingling. On the construction site, if you smelled a fart, you immediately asked the person if they shit their pants. As a matter of fact, I did shit my pants. Do you like it? I miss those conversations.

Going into that office was a major culture shock. I went from spending my lunch breaks exchanging nude picture texts of last night's hottie to looking at pictures of thirty-year-old women's babies. No, your baby is not cute. And why are you telling me you're proud of your baby walking? Aren't all humans supposed to walk? That's like saying the sun rose today. Only inform me of your infant's achievements if it's dunking a basketball or bench pressing a sick amount of weight. I never thought I'd miss looking at the pics of hairy, beat-up catcher's mitts that my construction compadres were throwing their junk into.

My white-collar lunch breaks are a prime reason why working in an office sucks. It's because women work at offices. I have nothing against women in the workplace. But biologically, women are not funny. Nor do they find humor in funny things. Science has proven that. The only time women are funny is when they attempt to swing a golf club or shoot a gun.

Everything is offensive to women. On the construction site, if someone is slacking off, you tell them to hurry their fat ass up. No one is offended. Say that to a woman in the office and you're looking at a verbal warning. You may even get, gasp, a written warning. What are we in, elementary school?

That's the thing about the office: you're walking on eggshells. I love the brutal honesty that makes up a construction site. If I fuck up, I am told that I am the dumbest motherfucker on the face of the planet and that I should get my shit together or fucking die. Now those are clear, straightforward words that I can easily interpret. Stop fucking up or take a nap on the freeway.

My first summer pouring concrete I didn't know anything. So, naturally, I fucked up every minute. Whether I cut the cord off the saw cutting wood, backed a cement truck into a house, or spilled a wheelbarrow of fresh cement on someone's lawn, I was always getting my head screamed off. But that's how I learned. Who needs to play twenty-one questions about shitty stuff you have to do every day, just to spare people's feelings? Gag me.

When I fucked up at the office, it was handled through a series of e-mail exchanges. They use positive reinforcement and passive language to get their point across. The first sentence will be, "First, I just want to say that you are doing a great job." Fuck off. I took the same business communications class that you did. You think that I don't know that trick of how to sugar-coat the bad news? Then it will say, "In the future, you should think about using the sticky note tool in Adobe when making notes on your work. It's easier to find your notes when I review it." Oh, okay, using a text box is a big-time fuckup? My bad. Fire me now. But what the hell do you want me to do instead? Now I have to get up and walk to your cube for clarification. I would rather kill myself than do that because your cube creeps me out with all the pictures you have of horses and cats pinned to your wall. The fact that you work all day in a box surrounded by cats dressed in human clothes is weird. If I politely say, "Hey, I got your e-mail, so you want me to use sticky notes from now on?" I might as well have pulled out a gun and asked for all her money. She immediately smiles with her mouth only and says, "No! I'm not saying you have to. I'm just saying that most people use them." How can I convey to her how much more effective it would be to simply e-mail, HEY DUMBASS, STOP USING TEXT BOXES; USE THE STICKY NOTE ON YOUR WORK? That's it. Problem solved.

I would never dream of sharing any hurt feelings with the human resources lady. I don't understand who actually goes to an HR person when they're feeling down. How gay is that? Could you imagine if I went to share my feelings at the construction site? The construction HR guy would show his empathy by having me do a therapeutic exercise. The exercise would be punching me in my head so that the physical pain from the punch outweighed my emotional pain. People just need to grow a pair.

There is one positive to the white-collar world. It's the fact that you don't have to look over your shoulder every five minutes wondering if a prank is being pulled on you. The worst prank that can happen to you is like when you stare at the screen for fifteen minutes trying to fix your frozen computer and shaking your mouse around until you finally figure out that someone has covered the LED with a Post-it note.

In the blue-collar world, there are no rules for pranks. If you leave your Coke sitting out, someone will dip their chew into it. If you leave your boots out, someone will put glue in them. If you leave your car unlocked, you may find a piece of roadkill on your front seat. You are most vulnerable when trying to take a shit in a Porta-Potty. There are multiple variations, but the grossest prank is called "blue butt." While you're sitting there, somebody grabs some rocks and drops them down the air vent. The rocks hit where all the shit is floating in blue chemicals and splash up your ass. If they want to be really mean, they have a buddy nail the door shut. There's nothing worse than being trapped in a Porta-Potty that has been baking in the sun all day with someone else's shit on your ass. It's almost as bad as taking a shit in the outhouse and realizing there's no toilet paper. Trust me, it sucks working the rest of the day without socks (if you get what I'm saying).

I can imagine that the office used to be a fun place to work. Pranks and jokes were probably the norm. But then women came in and ruined all the fun with their sensitive feelings and menstrual mood swings. Think I'm kidding? During my time at the office, I went on a couple of engagements. One was with all women, and the other with all men. Guess which one was more fun?

The engagement with the women was all business. No joking around, and we worked in complete silence. The only time we talked was to discuss something one of them learned in church, a coupon for the grocery store, or how they decided to put their kids in a private school. Yuck.

The engagement with the men was like "shooting the shit" with all your room-mates back in college. It was common for our discussions at work to include quotes from *South Park*. If I had blurted out, "Screw you guys, I'm going home" on the female engagement, not only would it be considered offensive, but they would have no idea what I'm talking about. Again, biologically women don't understand humor.

I'm not saying women shouldn't be allowed to work. But men were there first, and women should adapt to the culture that was established. It's like women put on their Christopher Columbus pants and made the men sit through sexual harass-ment and acceptable Internet usage seminars like they were on a missionary trip converting Indians to Christianity. And by converting, I mean forcing.

If I moved to France, I wouldn't expect them to speak English. I would buy Rosetta Stone and learn fucking French. So, if you're a female and I walk into your cube and crop dust the shit out of it, don't get offended. Instead, smile, give me a high five, and say "good one." If you allow that, I'll put up with listening about how you prefer pads over tampons. See, that's called a compromise. You give a little to get a little.

Even though women are the reason I hate working in an office, they're also the reason I love working in an office. For every ten fat or old women working there, there's one hot girl. Being able to look at a nice set of jugs is a great break in your day. There's just something insanely sexy about a hot girl in business casual attire. It definitely beats having to stare at an old man's hairy ass crack all day on the construction site.

I always got a kick out of seeing the ugly women in the office resent it when the male managers and partners gave the hotties more attention. It probably brings them back to the playground when all the boys would pick the hot girls first for a phys ed team. We all knew they weren't getting picked for their athletic ability. They were picked because their shorts were two sizes too small and their boobs jiggled up and down when they ran.

Women are resentful of good-looking girls no matter what level of society you're in. Look at the top level of America. Sarah Palin gets hated on because she's better looking but also gets all the attention. Maybe Hillary would get that attention if she lost the man suit and opened the blouse up a little more. On second thought,

Hillary, don't trade your man pants for a skirt until you hit the gym. No one wants to see your hail damage and cankles. That might start World War III while you're on your foreign diplomacy tours.

But don't get me wrong, there are plenty of guys in the office who will get on your nerves. True, men don't have the same cattiness as women. Guys can get along with any other guy. Even if you despise the guy, you can still block that out and finish whatever work that needs to get done. What I hate are the guys who are wieners. The ones that are socially awkward, sit down to pee, and play everything by the book. They will not stray away from the lessons learned in business etiquette courses they took in college. It's turned them into politically correct robots who use boredom as their lethal weapon. Even the Terminator has no chance of saving John Connor from that. The wieners have been this way their whole life.

These are the guys in elementary school who had their initials on every crayon, pencil, and piece of clothing they owned. In high school, they would make the multiple folder barricades on their desk so no one could copy their exam. When they got to college, they raised their hand to ask a question every five minutes in a general class in a giant lecture hall. This isn't your major, why do you care about Freud's id, ego, and superego? I had to put up with this type of guy my whole life, and now that I've graduated college, he's in the cube next to me. Son of a bitch.

At work, this guy will try to weasel around you in every way he can. Let's say you're in a meeting with the boss. The boss asks how much work is left to be done. You raise your hand and say there are forty workloads left. The wiener's hand will immediately shoot up and correct you: there are actually thirty-seven workloads left. My fucking bad. Let me correct myself, there are approximately forty workloads left. You little dipshit. It doesn't stop there. That wiener will revolve his life around being a timecard superstar and making sure he shows up a half hour earlier and leaves a half hour later than you. What a cock-smoke. To counter the wiener's obsession with the time clock, you have to make your schedule unpredictable. Randomly show up an hour earlier, and bet your life savings that he will show up an hour and a half earlier the next day. I'd be able to retire right now with those odds. The wieners at the office are really the only weird people you're going to encounter. They suck. But at least they are predictable, and you have someone to fuck with. Jim vs. Dwight in *The Office* is right on the money.

On the construction site, it's a whole other story. Most of the guys who do blue-collar work are normal, everyday dudes. But the chances out there of working with a really unique character are quite high. Until I began pouring concrete, I didn't know people like this existed.

Every morning I'd show up at the job site and receive a picture text of this one crew member's morning shit. I'd be waiting in my car, see the guy was leaving the Porta-Potty, and hear my phone beep. I'd open it up to see a big brown mess. What the fuck, dude? The sad part is that this guy's mind wasn't even all that twisted, in comparison.

I was working with this fifty-year-old guy who wore sweat pants to work and didn't believe in deodorant. Unfortunately, his low hygiene was not what made him unique. On Monday morning, I inquired about how his weekend went. I expected a man of that age to go into detail about how he cut the lawn or watched NASCAR all Sunday afternoon. Nope. He casually said that he woke up Sunday afternoon in his parents' basement with a vibrator still turned on in his ass after a night of illicit drug use. I didn't pursue any more details. That same guy also confessed his passion for fucking a deer's heart after he shoots one on a hunt. Apparently, the texture and warmth of the heart feels like a vagina. That takes *American Pie* to a whole new level. Whatever happened to a bottle of Jergens and a tissue?

Hearing stories of guys fucking animals was not that uncommon, believe it or not. For some of the guys who spent their adolescence growing up on a farm, one could find the lady of the evening in a short walk over to the sheep pasture. I guess when the nearest person is ten miles away, that little ewe starts to look more and more attractive. But, goddamn, if you're that desperate, sit on your nondominant hand until it goes numb and give yourself a "stranger." If that doesn't do it for you, I suppose you could warm up a cantaloupe in a microwave and cut a hole in it. I'm not saying I have; I'm just saying that I could find plenty of ways to replicate a woman other than smacking a sheep's ass. But that's just me.

In the white-collar world, in addition to the stories you hear, you're going to receive plenty of advice from the older men. People love to share their knowledge and experiences and hand out practical advice. It may come in the form of a stock tip or a new grip to improve your golf swing. These are things that you can actually use. On the construction site, the advice you receive is more what not to do.

During one lunch break, I had a slight cough. One of my fellow concrete pourers decided to share his medical knowledge. After he diagnosed my ailment, he prescribed meth. He said that meth heals you because, once you take meth, you don't have the flu anymore. I can see his logic—you won't feel a goddamn thing, much less a sore throat. You could also prescribe meth for a severed limb. You won't notice your arm is gone while you are bleeding out.

Rick James had it wrong. Meth is a hell of a drug, not cocaine. I never met a meth head that I didn't like. Sure, they're crazy and I'd never let them around children, but they work a million miles an hour. The best part is that they will do any task you give them because they are so paranoid you'll know they're high. I strongly feel we could have saved millions of dollars in damages to the Gulf states if we'd sent a pack of meth heads down to the Gulf with straws. The oil spill would have been sucked up in one day. It would have cost BP only a carton of cigarettes per meth head.

White or blue? In the white-collar world, you take the advice; in the blue-collar world, you take the advice by not following the advice. I'm fluent in both schools of thought, and I think they equally helped me on my life journey.

Now the really tough question is, what environment do I prefer to work in? In one, you will get skin cancer and break your back all day and turn into Christopher Reeve. In the other, you will go blind and have your spine morphed into Quasimodo from hunching over a computer all day. Either way you're going to end up a crippled slave.

I always found it amusing that every blue-collar guy wishes he had gone to college because he hates manual labor and believes he is digging his own grave with every turn of his shovel. At the same time, every white-collar person hates their boring job and thinks about creative ways to commit suicide with their Ethernet cord. So where does that leave me?

I wish I could combine the shenanigans of the blue-collar world with the comfort of an office. That place is where I would want to work for the rest of my life. So, Johnny Knoxville, if you're reading this, please consider this book my résumé. I think I could make a great addition to the Jackass Headquarters. The ball is in your court, Johnny. I shall await your decision.

NEVERLAND

I'm not talking about child molestation in this chapter. Neverland is now synonymous with raping little boys. I'm talking about Peter Pan's Neverland. It's a place where you go to forget everything that's going on in the world. A place where real life doesn't happen and all your wildest dreams can come true. My Neverland is where all my college bars were located, the legendary Water Street.

Water Street is a historic thoroughfare in the town of Eau Claire, Wisconsin. By day, there are families outside on café patios enjoying lunch and old ladies dressed in their Sunday best sipping tea after church. You would never suspect the cute little street to be the epicenter of drunken debauchery. But come nightfall, all the creatures come out to play.

I've partied in a lot of towns and states, and I keep coming back to Water Street. I can't explain why. But I'm sure everyone feels that way about their favorite watering holes. I feel at home there. It's like *Cheers*. What I love about Water Street is its ethos: If you're not buzzing by 7:00 p.m., you should see a doctor. There may be something seriously wrong with you. And for the health of the other patrons at the bar, please leave, because we don't want to catch your sober germs.

Now I realize this street may not be for everyone. If you prefer to limit yourself to a single appletini and plan on being functional enough to drive your Saab home, then you may want to spend your evenings elsewhere. To my knowledge, I don't think the words martini or Saab have ever been uttered on Water Street. So, you may feel a bit uncomfortable when you're surrounded by Bud Light and people who can barely walk home. But as for me, I wouldn't have it any other way.

Any midnight, I can approach a girl, with my drink spilled down the front of my shirt and puke taste still in my mouth from rallying in the bathroom, and hit on her in a drunken language that no one outside of Eau Claire can understand. Normal. She will respond in the same slurred gibberish, be missing one of her heels, have no idea where her purse is, and then begin making out with me. Normal. It's that kind of class that makes up the Water Street bar population. And by no means is that an insult. It's the way we like it.

When I get "Water Street drunk" in a classier city like Minneapolis, I'm frowned upon. I must be having too much fun. Let's say I approach a girl in Minneapolis in the same condition just described. To her, I look like a zombie, and she runs for her life as if I'm going to feast on her flesh. Granted, I look, move, smell, and speak like I'm one of the walking dead, so I'm not surprised by that reaction. In Eau Claire, everyone is already infected with the drunken zombie virus, so they just say, fuck it, I'll make out with you. And no, zombies don't feast on brains. That's a myth. We prefer saliva and fruity lip gloss.

So how does one get infected with the zombie virus? Well, I think I made that obvious. You drink early, and you drink often. I'm going to warn you, though, you have to be willing to throw all obligations and responsibilities out the window. So what if you have to work in the morning? Your place of employment has a bathroom that you can puke in. Who cares if you have an exam in the morning? Show up in the same clothes that you wet your bed in last night.

I remember showing up to an exam and the girl next to me said, "You smell like alcohol and urine." She had a very keen sense of smell because that was 100 percent correct. Then I copied her exam. See, I don't stress about responsibility. I got a B on the exam. It all works out in the end. So next time you're unsure whether to stay in or go out, say fuck it, get your zombie on, and hope you sit next to someone smart the next day. That's how we do what we do on Water Street.

Much as I would like to make the claim, I realize that Water Street is not the craziest street in the world. I won't even try to claim that. It's probably like most college town bar scenes in the country. But I will claim that while bigger schools get the national attention for being party schools, I've noticed that the smaller schools seem to do it better. Or at least it feels that way.

In smaller cities, everyone has to go to the same strip of bars. So even if your college is only ten thousand people, they will all be at the same spot. You get to know everyone. At a college in a bigger city, all the bars are spaced apart from each other, and it doesn't have that same intimate feeling because the crowd at those bars changes every night. Since you don't get to know the people, it's harder to let loose and act retarded, mainly because people will think you are genuinely retarded or, in my case, a zombie.

You have to put your cool kid pants on to fit in at big-city bars. That's just not my style. At the larger colleges, the cool kids are the guys who go out in a sport blazer with an Ed Hardy t-shirt underneath it. No male should ever have that much glitter and rhinestones on an outfit. Let's get real. A high school girl bedazzling her homecoming shirt wouldn't even put on that much shirt-bling. In all honesty, if you want to dress like you're a Hollywood socialite, that's fine. But don't bring the attitude to match. Standing by the bar pretending to be contacting someone important on your BlackBerry is not as cool as when you saw it on *The Hills*. You look like a douche. You look like a bigger douche when all your Facebook pics from the bar show you making faces like you're a Calvin Klein model. If you have the presence of mind to make poses while you're drunk, I feel like you're actually sober and slipping roofline into everyone's drink. Pervert.

Now if you go on my Facebook, all my pictures look like I'm posing for the Special Olympics advertising campaign. If you placed me in a Special Olympics race at the moment those photos were taken, I'd get last place via not finishing. So if this sounds like your Facebook profile, too, let's go to Goodwill, pick out an outfit, and head to Water Street. You will feel right at home.

Water Street has ten bars on a two-block strip. The best part is that there are no covers, no lines to get in or to get drinks, and no drinks more than three dollars. I hate going to a big city, waiting a half hour to get in, and then waiting another half hour for a beer that costs six dollars. With all the waiting in line, you probably get ten minutes to actually roam about the bar. I need a whole lot more than ten minutes to convince a girl to come home with me. I need at least one hour, forty bucks, and an FBI hostage negotiator. Even if I wanted to hit on a girl in that pathetic ten-minute window, I probably would bump into a guy and spill my drink on him. In larger cities, that apparently is cause for a fight. Sorry, man, I didn't try. It's just that the DJ put on Lady Gaga's "Just Dance," and my body couldn't help but follow directions. On Water Street, everyone is too drunk to notice a spilled drink down their back. (Did you feel that? I think there's a hole in the roof.)

Most people reading this probably haven't been within a hundred miles of these bars, or ever will. That is irrelevant. The point is to appreciate the attributes that make me love these bars. The more weird, random, and dirty a bar is, the more likely I will frequent it. So, if you decide to come to Water Street, you will find me at one of three locations.

The first is Shenanigans. I like this bar for the dance floor. It's been real good to me. It's dimly lit enough for women to feel comfortable dancing with their boobies out. Who doesn't like boobies? The dark lights also conceal any heavy petting that may be going on. Although it can be a little weird having a chick's hand down your pants as a guy is grinding with someone else behind you having his ass rubbing against yours. But as long as you stay hole to hole, and don't go pole to hole, it's not gay.

My second location is the Brat Kabin. I really enjoy the aroma. There's not a better smell in the world than the exquisite blend of urine and Pine-Sol. At this bar, you can buy cans of Busch Light and PBR for one dollar. Maybe you're a bit classier than that and prefer a nice glass of wine. Well, go right up to the bar and order yourself a bottle of Boone's Farm. On second thought, don't. My experience with Boone's Farm had me bedridden for two days on nothing but Gatorade and Advil.

The third and most likely location to find me is The Pickle. This bar has one rule. No cock on the block. There's an elevated platform that girls dance on ("the block"). If a male decides to get up on the block and dance, the DJ will cut the music and tell him to get down. If he refuses, he will be shunned by everyone in the bar with the "asshole" chant.

I wish more bars would enact a "cock on the block" zero tolerance policy. No one wants to see some white guy trying to impersonate Usher. It doesn't work. You bring all white people back to the days of Vanilla Ice and the "horrible dancer" stereotype. "Ice Ice Baby" will haunt me forever.

There's always an event going on at The Pickle. *Girls Gone Wild* came to film there in my sophomore year. I was so excited. It felt like Christmas morning. However, when I arrived at the bar, it quickly turned into the same emotion you get after you open up all your presents and receive only sweaters and socks, i.e., the population of the bar was all dudes. In both cases, you say the same thing, "What the hell is this shit?" In hindsight, I shouldn't have been surprised. It's like going to a nude beach—no women there either. When I was in middle school, on a family vacation, I snuck over to the nude beach. I stepped over the ridge to receive a big eyeful of penises and one old lady who was letting the wind blow in her hair (both places). That nude beach was one of the most traumatizing experiences of my life. I think I ran home crying. I should have done the same thing at the Girls Gone Wild night. With no girls to see, I drank the entire bar, located a sheltering bush behind the bar, and passed out, only to be discovered by three cops.

Fortunately, my fake ID, expressly designed for such situations, saved the day. All three cops fell for it and gave me two options: they would call my ex-girlfriend to come get me or else they were taking me to cetox. I later learned from her that she found me sitting on the sidewalk, drooling and shouting to the police that I was nineteen. Smart. I also made a feeble escape attempt that was quickly foiled by me getting body slammed into the pavement. After all of that, she carried me home. Miraculously, I woke up the next morning with absolutely no tickets or fines. Hallelujah!

But why exactly did I go to the bar every weekend? It's interesting, if you think about it. I spent at least fifty bucks a night doing that. Why don't I just spend fifteen bucks on a case of beer and play Xbox all night? I'll tell you why: I can't stick my penis in my Xbox (I've tried). You're a hunter, and you go where the food supply is.

My friends and I even made a philosophy out of it. When you go to the watering hole, you look for the wounded one, or the baby of the gazelle herd, maybe wildebeests if you're desperate (usually I am). The wounded one is the girl who is just drunk enough to become a slut. The baby is the girl who has low self-esteem. If you can find the three-legged baby gazelle, you aren't going hungry.

I was (and still am) horrible at luring my prey. My tactic was to wait for a girl to come up to me. That never works. Do you ever see a gazelle walk up to a lion and ask, "Oh, hey, what's up?" Fuck, no. I don't care how long you can stand there flexing. And believe me, walking around and flexing isn't any sexier than C3PO's best moves. Not hot. If you want something, you got to go get it.

One of my roommates was a pro at applying our philosophy. Generally, he would get turned down ten times before he finally nabbed one drunk enough to say yes. Now that's what I call a "go-getter." Make something of yourself. If you can dream it, you can do it.

Keep in mind, if you get turned down by the first five, you need to lower the bar. You aren't going for the prize of the herd. It's about quantity, not quality. You don't need a Lamborghini to get from point A to B. A rusted-out Geo Metro with no suspension will still get you to your destination. The one and only instance where I'm against peer pressure is when your one buddy will pull you aside and be like, "Do you really want to go home with that?" Yes, I do.

This is the same guy who has a really hot girlfriend and can get laid anytime he wants. It's like he's living in America and I'm in Ethiopia. He gets to eat steak every goddamn night while I'm waiting in a bush with a spear for something to walk by and pounce on. I have no idea when the next meal is going to come. He has no right to tell me to pass on the hippopotamus. Pickers can't be choosers. You're not marrying the brawd, you're just looking for a lil' one-night companionship.

For me to actually bring a girl home, I need one of two things to happen: an act of God, or the perfect storm. I have yet to have the act of God happen. That's when you come home and walk into your room to find a naked angel in your bed beckoning you sweetly to lie with her. I still have faith that my prayers will be answered someday.

So I have to rely on the perfect storm. There are so many variables that have to fall into place to take a girl home. You have to meet her twenty minutes before bar time—the perfect amount of time to chat, dance, and do shots. Any less and she will pull, "I have to go to the bathroom. Wait here." She's not coming back. You then look like an idiot telling your buddies that you're waiting for this "mystery" woman.

The second variable that needs to happen is that her friends all left without her. This may be the biggest hurdle of all. A girl's friends are like the offensive lineman for a quarterback. Their job is to protect the quarterback from literally getting "sacked." The best pass rush is if her friends blow their blocking assignment and you have a clear path to the quarterback, i.e., they aren't around. If the linemen are there, you have to try and battle around them by buying them shots. Let's just say I usually get pancaked by the linemen. Game over.

If by some miracle the first two do somehow fall into place, the storm is definitely starting to brew. But you are by no means guaranteed that Hurricane Katrina will hit your bedroom. The walk out of the bar is important. Do not succumb to after-bar munchies. The linemen will most likely be there chowing down and can ruin your whole night's work if they see you with their quarterback. Simply ask her to A-bar ("after bar") at your place. It's a nonthreatening invite. Do not say, "What do you say we head back to my place?" That sounds the creep alarm in her brain, and there is no way she's coming back with you.

If she agrees, things are looking really good. Now, there is only one variable left, but it is the one variable that you can't control: the amount of alcohol she consumed. If she drank too much, she will puke all over your bed as soon as you take her shirt off. Kind of a mood killer. Stomach acid and Cosmopolitans are not an aphrodisiac.

Let's say the stars do align and she's in your bedroom, shirt off, not puking. Bring on Hurricane Katrina. Welcome to the Thunderdome. I love drunk sex. You last forever. It's like you are the Energizer Bunny. You last 1000 percent longer than the time I lost my V-card that was like 1.5 pumps totaling five seconds. I still don't get how it was that quick when I had three condoms on and shouldn't have been able to feel anything. The reason for fortifying my penis then was because health class had made me scared to death of causing a pregnancy. That class made me feel like you could get a girl pregnant just by sitting in the same room as her.

Even though you think you are awesome at sex when you're drunk, you're probably not. I would never want to watch a sex tape of me drunk fucking. I imagine the dialogue in the film would consist of comments such as: "NO. That's my belly button." "Are you still awake?" or even better, "Was that a fart or a queef?" There's nothing hot about drunk sex.

The morning after is always fun. Your solid 7 is now definitely a 2. Woof. Whether you fornicated at your place or her place, the morning shuffle always gets played. I hate this game. That's the one where you have to rescue your clothing naked in front of a stranger. No one needs to see my hairy ass in daylight. I always get the disgusted look. "Did I really do that guy last night?"

The most important pieces of clothing to locate are the boxers and thongs. If by chance you can't find them, you better hope to God there are no skid marks in those bad boys. Not only will you never be able to hook up with this girl again, but count out all her friends. No one will want to touch a guy now known as "shitpants." And ladies, that thong you were unable to find? It will be pinned to the guy's living room wall, crusties and all. So even though I hate to play this game, you have to, or you will never get laid in that town again.

The last phase is the walk of shame. A couple miles, in the sun, on a Sunday morning. You look like shit and feel like shit. The worst part is the sun. It hits you like you were underground in a bomb shelter for the past ten years. Makes you feel like you're inside an African's nutcup. Steamy. I feel it's God's way of punishing you for your night's sins.

Almost as bad is that all the families are out enjoying their Sunday morning. They probably just got out of church, and you're walking down the street as if you just climbed out of the depths of hell. The parents cover their children's eyes. This is definitely no Sunday stroll. It's a fucking death march. But it is just something you have to put up with to have a good night at the bar. Once you get home, it's Gatorade and making a nest in your bed for the remainder of the afternoon.

Whether you're on Water Street or somewhere else, we all do the same things at the bar. You get drunk and hope to get laid. That's it. Mammals will be mammals. If you analyze Mother Nature, every animal species is focused on one thing: getting laid. We aren't any different. If I stop going to the bar, I feel I will upset the natural balance of life. I don't want to be responsible for that, and neither should you. If we stop going to bars, life as we know it will cease to exist.

TEACH ME HOW TO BUCKY

Baaaaaaaah.Bah.Bah.Buuuh. WAAAAAAAAAAAAAAAAAAA!!!

That's my sorry attempt at sounding out the opening hook to House of Pain's classic single, "Jump Around." I wish you could have seen me trying to write that thing down. I was like a first grader trying to read Dr. Seuss for the first time. One fish, two fish, th-r-r…fuck this. Reading sucks. Is it time for recess yet?

For anyone not from Wisconsin, "Jump Around" is the anthem for anything Badger. It is played at every University of Wisconsin-Madison sporting event. I don't care if it's played at a funeral, those Madison people will get out of their seats and jump around. The song triggers "Badger" in their head. It's like saying the word "rocks" around a former crack-head. The town needs an intervention for the amount of Badger they shoot up.

I'm not concerned for them; I'm envious. It's hard to describe the Badger fever in Madison. Every Saturday during college football season you just know when it's game day. Aside from the town painted red, there's just something in the air. It's like when animals can sense a storm coming. There's a mixture of feelings, mostly sexual. The town gets wet for Bucky (the mascot). I'll admit it, even though I come from Minnesota, it was tempting to turn to the dark side and join the Badger nation.

On Gopher game day at the University of Minnesota, you show up at the game and you have to check your GPS to make sure you're in the right spot. It's like a ghost town. In Madison on game day, you have to check the calendar to make sure it's not actually New Year's. I've spent many weekends in Madison, and I have to say, it's quite the experience.

Whether it's game day or not, that town is always partying. UW-Madison is usually ranked high on the national party school lists. I've never visited the other big universities in the country that are ranked higher, but knowing what I know, I'd be scared to visit them. My brain can't comprehend what they could possibly be doing to be ranked higher than UW-Madison. They must have mass public orgies while taking LSD that lasts for weeks on end. Or they routinely have human sacrifices.

When it comes to Midwest colleges, big or small, UW-Madison has unique demographics. Not only does the campus attract the obvious Midwest population, but it also has a high number of East or West "Coasties" (most likely from the Northeast Coast). This addition creates a unique culture.

The Coasties that come to Madison are the ones whose daddies couldn't buy them into an Ivy League school. They then turn to the next best thing: UW-Madison. A lot of Midwesterners aren't fond of the Coasties. I, for one, am. I think it's a good thing that they take four years out of their life to come here and teach us backward people how to be civilized. Coming from a coast, they obviously know more about everything in life than those born in the flyover states.

However, it's hard to get the Coasties to share these life lessons with us. If they sense your Midwest roots, you will receive a grossed-out look and be promptly trampled over by their Ugg boots. They don't have time for the inbred Midwest folk. If you are dead-set to overcome your savage Midwest upbringing, then you must deceive the Coasties. You must make them think you are one of them. You have to dress like a Coastie, think like a Coastie, and behave like a Coastie. You will then be able to pick the Coastie's brain to achieve the total enlightenment that they possess.

To become a female Coastie, you need to don black Spandex pants, a v-neck t-shirt, and giant sunglasses. You should also have a side pony tail and wear a North Face jacket whenever the temperature dips below 60 degrees. Once fully outfitted, head immediately to Starbucks and get a coffee. With your mocha in hand, proceed to walk down the street talking on your BlackBerry. Don't forget the touches of realism. Act like you're going down the catwalk and get frustrated if someone is in your way. Throw out a "What the fuck" to anyone insensitive enough to not move out of your way. And most importantly, don't get caught socializing with a Sconnie (for idiots: Sconnie = Wisconsinite). That makes you look dirty and is grounds for expulsion from Coastie society.

To become a male Coastie, dress like you're going sailing on your yacht. To simplify this process, go to your local mall and buy whatever the manikin is wearing at the Polo Ralph Lauren section. I highly recommend wearing two polo shirts at once. Make sure to match the color of the Polo symbol on the top shirt to the polo you are wearing underneath. Then pop those collars and strut down the street like the baddest motherfucker on the planet. Nothing says badass like pastel-colored shirts. And keep this in your mind at all times: every single female wants your nutsack. Don't forget that.

Well, now that you're dressed like a Coastie, it's time to head out for the evening. Don't plan on going to house parties or college bars frequented by the hordes of local peasants. It's best to stick to Coastie Island, a strip of sororities and fraternities exclusive to your kind. It's a safe haven. I like to think of it as a Jamestown. Its purpose is to keep the savages out. I can't tell you what specifically goes on inside the walls of Coastie Island. But what I can tell you is, think high-class cocktail parties where everyone brings their own Tide to Go stick just in case someone spills a Grey Goose apple martini on them.

I have spent many days living amongst the Coasties in hopes of learning why they are so much better than every other person on the planet. They must have some secret, some knowledge to unlock eternal happiness that we in the Midwest don't quite possess yet. When my time came to learn this secret, I was thoroughly disappointed. It was like I had spent hours watching a shitty movie with an abrupt ending that pisses you off even more. Take the movie *Signs*. Really? H_2O kills the aliens? Fucking stupid.

The stupid secret to Coastie superiority is that they were born on the Northeast Coast. That's it. The geographic location of their birth makes them smarter, better, and more human than the rest of the population. When I found that out, I took off my Yankees hat and exposed my true identity. The Coasties couldn't believe that they were bamboozled by a savage. I was rushed out the door, and on my way out I yelled, "FUCK THE J-E-T-S, JETS, JETS, JETS." I have never returned to the Coastie Island.

In reflection, I would like to make a couple of points. If we are judging intelligence level based on your geographic location of birth, shouldn't the Coasties be considered retarded? They live in areas subject to hurricanes, earthquakes, crime, overpopulation, floods, and smog. If the ice caps truly melt, like the people of the Northeast Coast say, New England will be under water. Who looks dumb now?

When the caps melt, don't come swimming over to the Midwest asking for salvation. I'll remember the time you scoffed at me on the sidewalk, and I will then hold your head underwater with my foot. Based on geography and weather patterns, the upper Midwest is the safest place to live. Thus, using the Coastie logic of geographic settlement, the Midwesterners should be the smartest people in the country, for our ancestors settling here.

On the topic of ancestors, the Coasties are descendants of people who were too pussy to travel west during our country's expansion. While my ancestors were battling mountain beasts, Injuns, and rattlesnakes with their bare hands, the Coasties' ancestors were sipping tea and eating crumpets.

I'd rather be cut from the cloth of Minnesota's Paul Bunyan than...um, huh. There aren't any tall-tale characters from the Northeast. Pecos Bill, Davey Crockett, Johnny Appleseed, and John Henry are all from other parts of country. I wonder why that is? The answer is that no one wants to write about prissy East Coast statesmen who never left the comfort of their homes. Who's going to write a tall-tale legend about Sir Edward wrangling his knickers onto his legs? With our accurate history lesson established, can we play connect the dots? That's the only puzzle game I'm good at. Fuck Sudoku. So basically, the Coasties come from areas prone to natural disasters and descend from a lineage of prissy statesmen. The dots show that the Northeast people, including the current generation, are retarded pussies. So, Coasties, drop the stuck-up front. You're not fooling anyone anymore. Your poop is the same as my poop. If I can't send a bucket of my feces to Cash4Gold, neither can you.

I would like to apologize to the majority of the UW-Madison campus for starting off on a negative foot by introducing the Coasties first. That's never good. However, I didn't want them to receive any credit for the awesomeness that is the city of Madison. The Midwest population is like the heart of Madison's cardiovascular system. They make the party pump. The Coasties are like a blood clot. They just get in the way. So, when you make a pilgrimage to Madison, stay away from the blood clots—you might have a heart attack.

If you're looking for a good weekend to head to Madison, there's really no bad one. But to get the most bang for your buck, go for Halloween, or in the spring for the Mifflin Block Party. These two giant street affairs attract at least fifty thousand people. Shit goes down. YouTube both events. See for yourself. Seriously, do it now, bitch. I'm too lazy to go into detail about it.

I love the Halloween party because of the girls wearing slutty outfits. All they have to do is take any ordinary occupation and put the word slutty in front of it. What are you supposed to be? I'm a slutty firewoman. I'm a slutty lumberjack. I'm a slutty secretary. Easy. I have yet to see a slutty sanitation worker, but I think that has the potential to be super hot.

Guys, however, have to think outside the box. I can't pull off anything slutty. Nor would I want to expose humanity to that disgusting sight. One year, at the height of Mr. Vick's questionable treatment of canines, I wore his jersey and, with a giant stuffed dog on a noose, chanted "fuck dogs" down the street. That was a crowd pleaser.

If you're not a creative guy, you can go the "no costume" route and be like all the creepy old men who line the side of the street and videotape up all the hotties' skirts for new spank bank material. Either way, as much as I love the Halloween party in Madison, it doesn't have the spontaneous grassroots feel of a college party. It's too organized for my liking. So, if you want a giant dose of a real Madison college block party, go on down to Mifflin Street. And by giant dose, I mean like downing a bottle of painkillers. Death is a possibility.

Mifflin Street is completely lined with big houses, each one boasting three giant balconies filled with people. It kind of reminds me of Mardi Gras, but without the best parts, boobs and beads, which is unfortunate. I think we should make an effort to change that.

My first couple of years attending this party there was no alcohol allowed on the street. The minute you placed one foot on the sidewalk with a beer, you were zip-tied and forced to take the embarrassing walk to the mobile police station for processing, with people chanting "dumbass" at you. This prohibition made it somewhat hard for all the out-of-towners to get hammered. To get at a keg, you had to schmooze an owner of a house by claiming a mutual friend had invited you. This always sucked because the person's name that I was throwing out was like a fifth-removed cousin. You don't actually know the person.

You felt like a homeless person begging for change. C'mon man, help me out here. That was pretty much a waste of everyone's time. I found that trading my body got much better results. Now I know to just whip my wiener out immediately and say, "This is yours for a keg cup. Don't worry about being gentle."

I get the stinginess of the homeowners. The block is flooded with thousands of complete strangers. But at the same time, don't throw a party on Mifflin if you're going to be uptight. It's like putting a set of Legos in front of a little kid and telling him he can't build anything.

There was one time, during Mifflin '09, I experienced a particularly stingy homeowner. My buddy and I were chilling in a random backyard drinking out of the keg, and everything was cool. Then my buddy's bladder started knocking on the door. As he's peeing in the guy's bushes, the Asian owner of the house runs out onto his balcony and starts screaming down at us. He was upset about my buddy's penis being out. Since he was Asian, I'm assuming he was upset because he has a hard time seeing his own. I can see how that could be stressful. But why take it out on us? We politely apologized and said we would leave. He replied, "Fuck that" and started stomping down the stairs.

I decided to pull a George Bush and do a preemptive strike. I wasn't going to wait and get bicycle-kicked in the head by Lou Kang. I dropped my beer, met him at the top of the stairs, and launched him as hard as I could, like I was in the Royal Rumble. All I remember is seeing the Asian, and then, not seeing him. At first I was thinking, ninja? Then I realized the whole opposite side of the deck railing was gone. I did not expect him to be that aerodynamic and fly all the way through the balcony railing onto the ground six feet below. Maybe their eyes produce less air drag? At any rate, I was in shock and just stood on the deck looking down at everyone looking up at me. I felt like I had tripped over the power cord and cut all the music. Insert ASSHOLE chant. That was our cue to leave.

We made it back onto Mifflin Street and just started laughing, overcome by the ridiculousness of it all. Then all of a sudden I got pushed from behind. I turned around. It was the Asian, with an Indian buddy (dot, not feather). They started running their mouths, and at that point, my own mouth got the better of me. I compared them to Harold and Kumar. They pushed me again. I pushed them back. Enter the police, on cue. By now I knew the drill. They didn't have to say a word. I took out my ID and handed it to them. There was really no way to get out of this one. I admitted everything. I already knew I had the right to remain silent and dutifully put my hands behind my back. They escorted me to the station for processing. Let's just say my tax refund that spring went entirely to paying off the five-hundred-dollar disorderly conduct ticket.

Though I was still a little nervous the following year, I bravely went back. When I arrived on Mifflin, all my fears turned to pure joy. The city had lifted the ban on street alcohol. It was like I had just walked through the desert for days and found an oasis. I was so thrilled that I would no longer have to sell my body. I felt like Julia Roberts in *Pretty Woman.* I sprinted down to the liquor store, bought a case, and partied on the street all day long. It was glorious, and as usual, I loved every minute in Madison.

(Looking back at the whole college application process, I should probably have taken the time to write the extra essays to get into Madison after I was wait-listed for admission. But I am going to cut myself a break. My high school senior slide was in full effect at that time, and there was no way I was going to waste my precious party time on literary efforts.)

Madison is definitely the crown jewel of Wisconsin's university system, from both a party and academic standpoint. Hats off to them! They got it handled. I still proudly echo their inspiring slogans: Fuck Em', Bucky. Fuck You, Eat Shit. Teach Me How to Bucky. Jump Around.

On, Wisconsin!

ALWAYS LOOK BOTH WAYS

Everyone has that occasional night where they drank a little bit too much. You wake up in the morning feeling like an asshole. You're not really sure why or even what you did, but you feel like you should probably be hightailing it right over to the confessional. Your hypothesis becomes correct when you walk into the living room and one of your roommates simply says, "Do you remember what happened last night?"

I fucking hate that question. I get asked that a lot. You know there's never anything good that comes of it. The story your roommate tells you after he asks that question never involves finding a treasure chest of gold or bringing back a bunch of models to your house for a jumping jack competition. It usually involves you punching your best friend, defecating on public property, or getting thrown out of a bar. The question is a sure sign that you probably owe someone or something an apology.

One morning I woke up feeling like the biggest asshole in the world. Considering that I woke up in a hospital hooked up to a machine monitoring my vitals, somehow I just knew I had fucked up. As it turned out, I had been hit by a car as I was crossing the street. Seriously, who actually gets hit by a car? Don't answer that.

Let's rewind and recap the night's events, as in *The Hangover*. It was Halloween weekend. I had decided to stay in Eau Claire rather than go to the giant Halloween party in Madison. I figured I would stay out of trouble if I didn't go to that giant shitshow. Riiight. My friends and I decided to dress up for Halloween both Friday and Saturday night. I was dressed as Max from *Where the Wild Things Are*. My shirt said, "Where the Wild Thing Is," with an arrow pointing straight down. I totally made a sex reference! I am so cool, I know.

Friday night went on without a hitch. We went to the bar and got drunk. I even got laid that night. All I remember is playing rock, paper, scissors with the girl to see who had to go on top. Technically, I won, but she then pulled the card that we weren't going to bang if she had to go on top. Sore loser. So, eager to make the trip to tuna town, I hopped on top, and the whole time she kept making comments like "Hurry up," and "Are you done yet?" She just lay there, completely not into it.

Essentially, she lent me her vagina for five minutes to masturbate. That was nice of her. I wish more girls would do that. When I was done, all she said was "finally" and went to bed.

So, after Friday night, I was feeling pretty neat. I got my wiener touched by another human. You always have a little extra pep in your step from that. It's like you just broke into the vault, took what you wanted, and the next day the banker is left scratching her head asking, "How the hell did I let that happen? I am an idiot. And why does my vault itch?" Also as usual, the high from the heist didn't last long.

On Saturday, I had no idea that things were going to take a drastic 180. Isn't it funny how life works? One day you're getting laid, and the next day you've been hit by a car. I feel like that's a good life lesson. You can't control or predict anything, so party. If you had asked me on Thursday, I would have laughed and said no way in hell are either of those things going to happen. But life really is like a box of chocolates. On Friday, I picked the caramel-filled one, my absolute favorite. On Saturday, I got the coconut cream. Grossest flavor ever.

I really don't remember how I got into a makeout session with the grill of a car and ended up in that hospital bed. Thank God for Facebook. The next day pictures were posted. There I was at a Halloween house party, dancing on a table with a bottle of whiskey in my hand. The date stamp showed 9:00 p.m. That behavior usually comes out toward 1:00 a.m. I guess I hit it a little bit too hard, too early. But who could blame me? Getting laid is a rare occasion and therefore requires celebration.

After the dance routine, as my roommate tells it, we went down to the bar. I have to take his word on it. He became my babysitter that evening. Everyone has been the babysitter at one point or another. You have that one friend who can no longer function, and you have to make sure he doesn't die. In my experience, the fucked-up friend always wants more drinks, even though his neck can no longer support his head and he keeps landing face down next to all the empties on the bar. I usually order such friends a glass of water but tell them it's pure vodka. Works every time.

Well, that was me. All my roomie did was prop my lifeless body against a pillar in the bar. I was like a computer when it freezes up on you. I was still powered on, but nothing worked. You could shake me like a mouse all you wanted, and I wasn't going to respond. I think the critical window was flashing on my desktop saying, Windows has encountered a problem, low memory and battery life. Eventually, my automatic restart window popped up and started the countdown, right at bar time. My roommate had just dragged me out to the sidewalk when my hard drive suddenly rebooted and I could move on my own. Thank you, automatic update.

The pizzeria across the street was in my field of vision as I powered back on. I took off in a sprint with visions of delicious mac and cheese slices dancing in my head. Always look both ways when crossing the street. Every kindergartner knows that. Apparently, my common sense was still in preschool. My roommate said that he saw the impact coming a mile away.

I like to describe the incident as akin to the time when Randy "The Big Unit" Johnson threw the pitch that exploded the bird flying past the pitching mound. Like the bird, I was oblivious. And like the ball, the Toyota Camry was coming in hot. POOF. There goes Thomas.

The crown that I was somehow still wearing for my Halloween costume flew twenty feet, again, according to my roommate. The car then sped off. He was probably drunk, too, but because I was in the middle of the block and not the crosswalk, he was not at fault. He could have stopped with no problem. Now he has felony charges of fleeing an accident. Dumb fuck.

I stood up in shock. I mean, shock is a given when you get smoked by a car. But standing up was a bonus. If you want a real good way to sober up, have your buddy ram you with a Camry. A million bystanders all came running over to me. I vaguely remember one bitch saying that she's going to school to be a nurse and was trying to tell me what to do. It was all generic advice. Be calm. Sit down. Take deep breaths. No shit, bitch. Thank you for your help, but I probably know just as much as you from watching *ER*. Now get away from me.

The real paramedics soon arrived and tried to force me to get in the ambulance and go to the hospital. I felt fine, so I refused. I think that my drunk body must have been like a gel-filled Stretch Armstrong action figure. My limbs and body probably flew every which way, preventing any damage to them.

What I didn't know is that I had a gash on my forehead and was bleeding down the side of my face. By law, they were required to take me to the hospital. They wanted personal information. What's my name? Fuck if I know. Where do I live? Who the fuck knows? The concussion wasn't really helping my drunk brain.

They called one of my other roommates who had stayed in that night from partying because he was sick. God bless his heart, he came to the hospital and stayed with me all night. However, my antics there only intensified. (Sorry, buddy!) Let's just say the entire ER staff earned their paycheck that night. I hated the forcible confinement. I kept questioning the credentials of the doctor and nurses. I was yelling and swearing at everyone. When they put me through the CAT and full-body scans, I was hitting the machines trying to wiggle out of the tunnels. I wish someone had taken a video. Watching a drunk guy freak out as the bed starts moving into the CAT scan hole like he's being slid into a cremation chamber would be viral video gold. After the scans, they brought me back to my room, and I ripped the vital sign sensors off my body. All the nurses came running in because they thought I had flatlined. I believe I said something along the lines of, "Good. Just checking your response time. You get a passing grade."

At this point, my roommate was still okay with calling me his friend. That all changed when I had to piss. The nurse came in with a bedpan, and I whipped out my genitalia and began to urinate into the bowl as she was holding it. The whole time I was staring at her face and repeatedly asking, "Do you like that?" I'm surprised the bedpan didn't "accidentally" slip out of her hands onto me. That's what I would have done to the creepy pervert if I were her. "Oh, so sorry. Did you like that?"

I think the hospital made a bad move when it let four nursing interns into my room to take notes. I felt like a lab rat. I didn't like it one bit and, of course, began to make fun of all of them. One of the interns was Asian. I quoted lines from Gran Torino quite a bit while he was in there. I feel bad about that. But still, "Get me another beer, Dragon Boy" just cracked me up.

Before you call me racist, if you haven't decided that already, shut up. I'm not. To me, racial attributes are like any other physical attribute. If I'm upset at someone, I'm going to call out their big nose, fat gut, or fucked-up teeth. In my book, it's the same as skin color, eye shape, and cultural dress. If anything, I'm consistent in the fact that I make fun of every single type of person. Therefore, I don't think any one type of person is better than another. I like to think of myself as a species-ist. I make fun of all humans. So my little episode with the Asian intern at the hospital was not directed toward all Asians, just him.

At this point, the hospital was getting fed up with me and stationed a security guard in my room. He was fat. You already know where this is going. I kept challenging his ability to catch me if I decided to make an escape attempt. My logic was simple, and I let him know my plan. If I could just slip past his cheeseburger-assaulting fingers, there was no way his fat ass was going to catch me down the hallway. I told him that I wasn't going to escape, but if I did, he couldn't stop me. Apparently, I just wanted to make that clear. Eventually, I gave up insulting the man's diet habits and passed out. I think the whole hospital finally breathed a sigh of relief. It was like a cranky toddler who had trashed his crib before finally crying himself to sleep.

I woke up the next morning in the hospital bed feeling like I got hit by a car. My hangovers usually feel that way, but this time I did get hit by a car. I was going through all the papers that the hospital gave me. One of them looked like a police citation. I called the nurse in and inquired what in the hell that was about. She simply said that the cops had issued me a jaywalking ticket. Well, if that wasn't the cherry on the fucking cake.

The ticket was actually called "Sudden Pedestrian Movement." I want to know why someone drafted a law labeled that. Was there a town meeting discussing how suddenly people were moving? What the fuck? I also wanted to know why the police officer had issued that ticket. While I was on the ground, struck by a car, did he just waltz over, pull out his pen, and be like, yep, sudden pedestrian movement, place the ticket on my chest, and walk away? I mean, I get why I got the ticket. Rules are rules. But c'mon, man, use some discretion. Tickets should be used to teach a lesson. I think I already got that "sudden pedestrian movement" concept covered.

I decided to go to court about my ticket. For anyone that's been to court, you know the drill. There are about twenty people scheduled at one time, and you wait in a room for the judge to call you up and read your violations in front of everyone. When it was my turn, the judge said, "Apparently, you were drunk and got hit by a bicycle or vehicle of some sort."

I replied, "It was actually a Camry, your honor." I could hear the giggles coming from the peanut gallery behind me. Even the judge chuckled. You know you're an idiot if the judge can't keep a straight face. He decided to schedule me a meeting in a couple of weeks with the district attorney to negotiate my violation. The DA basically told me to fuck off and that I had no case/defense, on the grounds that I am an idiot. Can't argue with that. I pleaded guilty, which nipped in the bud my once promising prospects for a career as a defense attorney.

When it was all said and done, I paid two hundred dollars for the sudden pedestrian movement violation and around six thousand dollars for the hospital stay. Whatever. Now, I definitely look both ways when I cross the street. Hey, better late than never. If you see me at a crosswalk and I look like a little kid debating whether or not to jump in a pool, please don't make fun. I am a little gun-shy on that subject these days. Just give me ten minutes and I'll get there.

I'd also like to take the time to thank the staff at the hospital for putting up with my obscene bullshit. There are no excuses for the way I behaved. I know you knew I was drunk. I also appreciate the way you overcame the temptation to put cyanide into my IV. This is not a knock on the care I received, but I hope that I will never need your services in the future.

I'M THE LEAST YOU COULD DO

I've spent most, if not all, of my time in this "novel" discussing trying to hook up with girls and rolling the dice in the STD crapshoot. Even though it pains me to admit it, I have to come clean. Every dude eventually wants that one special girl. I feel I need to redeem myself with the entire female population before I completely alienate myself from them. I am not advocating that dudes should drop their sexual roaming tendencies. That would make me a hypocrite. But after you rack up a respectable amount of notches on the old belt, a more permanent option is desirable.

A good time to start looking for "the one" is around the time when you are no longer in college and your mother cuts you off. You need someone to do her duties. Those clothes won't wash themselves, a chicken won't jump in the oven on its own, and unless you have one of those robotic vacuums, your room is not going to magically be clean. Without my mother, I would have died of starvation or succumbed to hazardous living conditions many years ago. As I am writing this, I am rapidly approaching the cutoff date. I'm scared. I feel like the weatherman is predicting no rain for the next year. Famine looms. That's why I need a girlfriend.

In addition, it would be nice to have a permanent girl where you know her lady parts are clean. I've lucked out on pulling the trigger in Russian roulette long enough. Eventually, I'm going to get the bullet and have a cauliflower growth off the side of my ween. Your chances of meeting a nice girl at that point are slim to none. You're damaged goods. The search for a life mate is now narrowed down to dirty women who frequent truck stop bathrooms because you'll share one thing in common. Cauliflower.

Before you condemn me and conclude that I believe a woman's role in society is to do everything for me short of wiping my ass, let me speak some logic into your head. You see, if you can find a girl who's willing to take care of your basic needs as a living organism, she will get anything she desires. Women actually have all the power. If I don't do what she says, I don't eat or get sex. Therefore, I am chained to her every whim and call.

I don't know why more girls don't take advantage of this superpower. They literally have mind control. Girls can start using this power even before you date them. If I meet an attractive girl at the bar, and she seems interested in me, I'm doing whatever she says. I'm like a jester for a king. All she has to do is clap her hands and say, "Dance, jester boy." I will be hopping around the bar looking like a fool just to make her happy. It's completely beyond my control.

If I were a girl, I would use my powers for evil and make guys at the bar do ridiculous things for me. I'd walk up and say "You're cute," to reel the guy in. Then I would ask for a drink. As I'm sipping my drink, I'd tell the guy to pull down his pants and get on the bar for my personal entertainment. If he refused, I'd call him gay and tell him I'm going to find someone more fun. My bet is that the guy is now hypnotized and will start teabagging everyone's drinks. Idiot. After that delightful showing, I'd walk away and say thanks for the drink and never speak to him again.

But, ladies, if you're actually interested in the guy, use your powers for good. Do everything I just suggested, except don't make him dunk his junk into people's drinks. An attractive girl can get laid at the bar by any guy she wants. That is a fact. But if you want more than a one-night stand, here's how you do it. You should still go home with him to show that you're interested, but you don't have to sleep with him. All you need to do is show an act of good faith. Give him a preview of things to come.

There's nothing worse than the girl who goes home with you every weekend for a month and does nothing with you. She usually says, "I'm really into you, but we aren't doing anything." You're reeled in because she also texts and Facebook chats you 24/7. She thinks by being celibate that she's making you want it more. Well, let me tell you, getting blueballed five weekends in a row is not a turn-on. Not only are you keeping me from being able to scope out new prospects at the bar, you're not allowing me to rub one out because you're staying the night. That's just rude.

If you really want a guy as boyfriend material, let him run the first-base line and maybe round halfway toward second. Allow him to swipe the two-finger credit card to see if he accepts or declines. I guarantee you will have him right where you want him. Drag out not having sex a couple more weeks and hang out with him so he gets to know you better. By the time you're ready to have sex, you will both know whether or not you two would be the next Bonnie and Clyde. If you guys aren't compatible, then don't sleep with him. This way you keep it classy and both of you feel like it was worth a try.

If you both are interested after hanging out, bang him. That seals the deal. I would never date a girl who held out on sex. Would you buy a car without test driving how it handles? Does a gynecologist make a diagnosis without doing a Pap smear? Would you sign a mortgage without scoping the house out? Of course not. I'm not locking into a long-term loan with the girl unless I know the ins and outs of the property. I don't want to move in and then find out down the road that her basement has a mold problem.

If the home inspection checks out, and everything is up to code, let's make it Facebook official. Send me the relationship request. It officially takes you off the market, and now the whole world knows it. There is not any gray area of whether or not you're with someone because by clicking "accept," you just signed the contract on the boyfriend/girlfriend dotted line.

Once it's official, this is the time where the woman's superpowers escalate to another level. It's Jedi-like. She waves her hand, and you turn into a drone. She is no longer just making you do things for entertainment purposes; she now controls everything you do in your social, physical, and personal life. Say good-bye to everything you once did. Trade in your Xbox for watching *The Bachelor.* Clean out your freezer of frozen pizzas because you will be put on a strict tofu and salad diet. You also better start enjoying walks and browsing produce at the local farmers' market. That is going to be your new Saturday morning instead of nursing your hangover.

The worst is going to the mall with your girlfriend. You will have two, and only two, duties when you're there. Duty number one is being a human clothes rack. All the items that she uses your money to buy will be your responsibility to hold and watch as she browses the department store. This duty is non-negotiable.

Duty number two is to be the judge of approval for everything she tries on. I say "approval judge" because there is no way you will disapprove of anything she tries on. She's like Kim Jong Il. You can't disagree or you will be beheaded. This sounds like a horrible life, doesn't it? Why would any man stoop to such levels?

Survival. We accept our trained and controlled life like dogs. Have you ever seen an asshole pet owner kick his dog, and yet, even though the dog is beaten, it keeps coming back? That's how guys are. We put up with the humiliating and oftentimes feminizing treatment of our girlfriends for two reasons: food and sex. The dog keeps taking swift kicks to the gut because it knows it will starve if it runs away.

I know that if I disobey my girlfriend I will be jerking off for the next three months and be eating TV dinners. So when she asks me to pick up feminine products at the grocery store, I gladly accept, with a smile on my face.

For me, I'm delaying my inevitable fate as long as I can. I'm like the Alamo. But as I said before, I'm currently on death row and awaiting my last meal from my mother. When it's finally my time to walk the green mile, only then will I surrender and let some woman carry my balls in her purse for the rest of her life.

I do feel bad for her. Without a doubt, I will be the least she can do. That statement is not because I have a low self-esteem. It's because I'm a realist. There will be no childhood dream come true of a princely knight in shining armor sweeping her off her feet onto a white steed. Rather, it will be the village idiot who passed out on the side of the moat with his own by-products dripping down the front of his shirt. I don't know any girls with that particular fairy-tale fantasy.

I already know that it's going to take a very, very special woman to tolerate me. I do believe she's out there. However, I do not believe that there is "one" person that is meant for everyone. If you look at it from a statistical standpoint, that would mean my "one" is most likely an Asian living in China because China has the highest population. I can tell you right now, I have no intention of ever going to that country. Not so much because it is communist, but more so because I'd rather not contract the bird flu. So that throws that whole "one" idea right out the window.

I do think there's a type of person for everyone. Multiple people can fit your type, not just one. I really have no idea what kind of girl would fit my type, but I imagine patience would be at the top of her attribute list, closely followed by a high tolerance for stress.

To give a snapshot of what she will have to put up with her whole life, I am already declaring that at our wedding I am coming down the aisle to Stone Cold Steve Austin's entrance music. And that's the bottom line. So if any ladies out there can handle my prerequisites, and have nice boobs, look me up on Facebook. I'd really like to get to know you.

If not, there's always my fallback plan. Mail-order bride. In all honesty, this will probably be my most likely route. I'd love to have a Russian bride who looks like a model and can't speak English. I don't care if she uses me to get citizenship. I get a super-hot chick who can't tell me what to do because I don't speak her stupid language. Perfect. It solves all my problems. She takes care of everything for me, looks hot, and I get to keep my balls due to the language barrier.

So, when you see a dazzlingly gorgeous six-foot blonde carrying my drunk ass home from the bar, just know that Ivana and I got through the citizenship process and are married happily ever after…well, at least I am. She's probably not. I'm now the best that she could do, AND she had no choice in the matter. I bought her. Gotta love it.

WE FESTING

One of my absolute favorite pastimes is attending concerts. I love seeing a musician live. I've been to shows in all types of musical genres. If you ask me the next day how the show was, I will always respond, "It was probably good." That's because every single show I've I gone to, I've been bombed. I couldn't tell you if a band or DJ was playing in between sets. Not a single detail. I'm okay with that.

I go to concerts for the party. (Surprised?) I'm usually at the very back of the crowd where seeing the performers on stage is nearly impossible. It's not because I don't have good tickets; it's because that's where the bar is. I hate having to fight the crowd every time I need to get another beer. People tend to cram the stage area as if they're in a third world country and the lead singer is throwing out bread. I'll pass on being a human sardine. The worst are the people who don't want to lose their position in the crowd by going to the restroom. Getting twenty feet closer to the stage is not worth the nastiness of feeling someone else's warm urine running down your leg.

Also, hanging out in the back is great for people watching. Since I can't see what the artists are doing on stage, my concert memories revolve around all the different types of people that our wonderful Lord has created. God has a fantastic sense of humor. I imagine he just gets bored and creates a bunch of weirdos to laugh at all day. I would.

Hard rock shows are the best. They raise all sorts of fascinating questions, such as how and where these people are employed to afford the tickets. It has to be at the circus or as an extra in a Tim Burton movie. One time, I was at a Korn concert in the middle of July. I could have sworn I got the date mixed up and it was really Halloween. And believe it or not, I was actually more entertained by the crowd's behavior than their costumes.

You already have to have a pretty low IQ to look in the mirror and think that an all-black outfit accompanied by a spike dog collar around your neck looks good. But to then jump in a mosh pit and beat the shit out of your already too few brain cells? That had me speechless. I know you're trying to take out your built-up aggression caused by your parents not hugging you enough as a child, but do you realize how stupid you look flinging your arms around with a bloody gash down your forehead? Watching these fuckers beat the shit out of each other was better than a UFC match. At least in the mosh pit it was all haymakers and none of the gay wrestling grapples that consume the majority of time in UFC bouts.

Don't forget that I was all liquored up. My remaining functioning brain cells needed a piece of the mosh pit action. So, when in Rome, do as the Romans do. I'll admit it, I was too pussy to actually go into the middle of the tornado. I stood on the edge and pushed people back in as they tried to exit the cluster-fuck. I'm an asshole. It was all fun and games until the giant bruiser of a man saw me doing this and decided to gore me like a bull in the streets of Pamplona. That son of a bitch sent me flying ten feet back onto the concrete floor. That was the end of my moshing days and attending hard rock concerts. I don't need to pay eighty bucks for a ticket to get my ass kicked. I can usually get that accomplished on any Saturday night at the bar for free.

The second concert genre I have abandoned is hip-hop/rap. No injury fears there. You'd think due to the violent nature of rap song lyrics that you'd have a higher risk of injury. False. The only people who can afford tickets to these shows are pussy, suburban, white kids, none of whom are packing any heat or boasting a gang affiliation. As much as these kids try to embody the gangsta image by dressing like Master P, they can't escape the fact that their mother dropped them off in a minivan. Totally white, totally not "hood," no matter how much Ecko and Fubu you put on. Dipshits. Go kill yourselves, you're embarrassing.

I don't mind rap on my iPod, but listening to it live is horrible. There's a reason no rap artists have live albums. On stage they sound worse than an immigrant trying to sing an English song at a karaoke bar. The entire set is comprised of the main rapper, plus ten of his homies jumping around waving towels while shouting out random words at random times, while the DJ in the background dropping the beat just keeps pushing play. Why did I just pay a hundred dollars to watch this, again?

The only concerts worth my money are country shows. I'm not talking about the giant extravaganzas played in a stadium. Those shows suck dick. I'm talking about the five-day-long festivals where you camp. My festival of choice is We Fest in Detroit Lakes, Minnesota. Shit gets weird there. The best part about We Fest is that all the people who attend the other types of concerts do not attend We Fest.

No wiggers, hippies, or Goths. That's my vision of America.

I like to think of We Fest as a sexual stat padder. If you were drafting people on your fantasy football team based on their sex number, you may use a late-round pick on me if you looked at my past year's total sex stats. However, almost all my points would come from that one very special weekend. Don't draft me. I'd be a bye-week replacement, nothing more. Everyone scores a couple touchdowns at We Fest, no matter how many scoreless weekends they have the rest of the year.

We Fest is all about free love minus the earthy, wookie-pussy, hippie chicks. I can handle a light landing strip or Hitler stache, but get that Chewbacca out of here. Thank God the girls at We Fest prefer the twelve-year-old look. If you can't get any action at We Fest, then you must be paralyzed and physically unable to do so. That weekend is seriously like a sex slave auction. All you have to do is point at a girl and say, "I want that one." The next thing you know you're getting laid underneath a trailer in the middle of the campground. Romantic.

I've spent many sleepless nights theorizing why these types of festivals guarantee you a chance at contracting herpes. I can tell you that it's definitely not that the people who attend these events are year-round Sex Feens. Almost all the girls who I've hooked up with at We Fest would tell me to go fuck myself if I tried to hit on them at a bar in the real world. And that, my friends, is the answer. The real world. You see, in the real world there are these things called rules and social norms.

So if We Fest isn't the real world, what is it? Well, have you ever seen movies that depict society in post-apocalyptic times? The ones where people forge shanty communities and live off scarce resources in a lawless world. That's We Fest. The campground residents have constructed makeshift bars, settlements, and clubs all over the place. People live off zero water, food, and sleep. Hygiene is far from proper. Even clothing is scarce in this world (both male and female). It's amazing how the human body can survive under these primal circumstances.

People get weird in this world. The only thing that keeps the population from becoming extinct is the bountiful alcohol resources. With one hundred thousand people clinging to life by keeping their BAC at a high level, superhuman survival abilities are activated. I like it. If this is what post-apocalyptic society is all about, Mr. President, please pick up the red phone and blindly launch every nuclear warhead in our arsenal. I'm ready to party.

Unwanted pregnancies and love bumps will be discovered a couple of weeks later. Don't let that deter you. It's still worth it. At We Fest parties the question is, what awkward and weird combination of activities doesn't happen? Think of the sex dice that you can buy at a sex shop. One die has a body part and the other has what you're going to do to that body part. You roll for a totally random result. That's the game played at We Fest, except the weirdness level gets multiplied by a hundred.

As soon as you wake up and exit your tent at 7:00 am, the dice are rolled. I usually find myself wearing only my special shorts, a style that no man should ever wear outside of We Fest. Any sudden movements or stretches will expose my junk to the world. I immediately start drinking and eventually head to one of the day-long dance parties. Along my journey to the party, I will acquire various alluring messages via Sharpie on my body to share with my world, like "show me where you poop from," or "tongue punch my fart box." Once at the party, things weird-up even more.

With the music blasting, there is no need for conversing with anyone. All you do is walk around thrusting your hips and rubbing your nipples. That is considered dancing and simultaneously how you communicate with people. Like monkeys. Mid-party you may find yourself colonizing a girl's wazoo with your fingers underneath her overalls. Or maybe a sixty-year-old woman comes by and decides to spank you with a fly swatter while she puts her index and middle finger on either side of her mouth and flicks her tongue in and out. I've even watched a buddy of mine get Cheez Whiz licked off his sphincter. Also, I hope you're okay with random flashes of boob, ball sack, labia, gooch, and ween. Those sightings are about as common as the rays of the sun. Just another party at We Fest.

Dear reader, are you slightly confused? Are you are left wondering, "What the fuck?" That's perfect because that's as close as I can possibly bring you to a true We Fest party feeling. And it's the best fucking time you will ever have in your life.

Have you noticed anything peculiar about my description of my favorite music festival yet? You guessed it, I haven't mentioned anything about the actual music. That's because you usually only go to one concert per day to take a breather from losing all of your bodily fluids. It's like a timeout for your penis. I call it that because it's much harder to hook up with someone when concert security is roaming the premises. Protect the innocent children in the audience and all that. Fucking party poopers.

In sum, I plan on going to We Fest every year until I die. I can see it now: At the ripe age of sixty, I will be setting up my single-person tent with my old, droopy balls hanging out of my XXL jorts. That chore done, the remainder of my week will be spent creeping out all my high school neighbors by sitting in a lawn chair with a sign that says, "show me your tits" as I drink myself into a coma. If I actually manage to be flashed a set, it will probably induce a heart attack and end my existence on Earth. On the bright side, I will have gone out doing what love. I wouldn't want it any other way.

That's because We Fest is all about being Young and Wild. Guys Like Me just need to have a Drink in Our Hand. Sure, you'll be Hungover and Hard Up when it's over, but that's Livin Part of Life. So, Homeboy, if you have a problem with this outlook, I suggest you just chill out and Smoke a Lil Smoke. Living my life this way Ain't Killed Me Yet and I don't see myself or Sinners Like Me changing any time soon. So, How Bout You?

IF IT'S A ROCKIN'
DON'T COME A KNOCKIN'

Whenever Hollywood advertises a new flick by calling it a summer block-buster, you know what to expect. The movie will have insanely high-tech special effects with explosions and plenty of action. You can also expect all the women in the film to be incredibly gorgeous and dressed in skimpy clothes. These elements are needed to outweigh the limited plot line. The good guys defeat the bad guys. The end.

A JMF Thomas story embodies this same beloved Hollywood reliability. There will be a combination of intoxication, a dirty sexual scenario, some element of danger, shit getting weird, or police intervention. This is followed by me calling my mother the next morning explaining why I need some type of assistance from her.

Those elements are my special effects. Thank God for them, or you'd be able to realize the actual plot of every single one of my stories never varies: got drunk, did something dumb, got in trouble. The end. There's not a better demonstration of my standard story makeup than one fine evening in the summer of 2010.

My friends and I had decided to rent a hotel room in a small town west of Minneapolis to attend a county fair. There was nothing special about this fair—rides, games, creepy carnies, and a beer garden. Standard.

Generally, I frequent county fairs to find washed-up older women. There's always at least one, wearing a cheetah print skirt from the '80s, divorced four times, and just wants her hole plugged. She plays musical chairs with every guy at the beer garden. If you're lucky, you get to be the last chair and go back to her double-wide and nail her.

But, unfortunately, this was not the reason I chose to attend this county fair. I went because a band called 32 Below was playing in the beer garden. I love this band. I love this band so much that I've been kicked out of every single one of their shows I've attended because I showed my love by getting passed-out drunk. This night would be no exception.

There were about twenty of us in our group, roughly a fifty-fifty mix of male and female. Once we got nice and toasted in the hotel, we all headed to the concert. I didn't think I would hook up with any of the girls in our group. They were either someone's girlfriend, someone I had known for a long time, or someone I already once hooked up with.

You'd think I'd have an "in" with one of the latter girls. False. I'm that one mistake on every girl's résumé. They don't make that mistake twice. I'm something that you would just rather have forgotten and never brought up again. It's like the public defecation ticket from your college days that you pray the recruiter doesn't bring up in a job interview. Pooping in the middle of the street will just never find a place in the corporate world.

When we arrived at the concert, I went straight to the beer garden. Essentially, I ordered a beer, pounded it, and got right back in line to order another. I was stuck on repeat. By the time the band got on stage, I was taxidermied. I looked lifelike, but nothing was alive or working on the inside. Typical.

About two songs in, it started to pour from the heavens. That is when shit turned weird. Everyone got soaking wet. As usual, the girls in our group started dancing around touching each other. It appeared that the rain had inspired them to play "Simon Says" with Mother Nature and have their own monsoons in their pants. The next thing I know I'm making out with a couple of them.

I felt like a ping-pong ball being volleyed back and forth between girls. Finally, one girl forfeited the match and didn't serve me back. She kept me all to herself. We continued to make out until swapping saliva wasn't cutting it anymore. We looked at each other, and then we looked at the Porta-Pottys sitting in the shadows off to the side. Two light bulbs clicked. Great minds think alike.

The next thing I know, I'm sitting on the toilet seat and she's jumping up and down on my lap like I'm Chris-fucking-Kringle. Someone's been naughty this year. Now, this wasn't the first time I've had sex in a bathroom or public place. But this was the first time I merged those two locations. And, for future reference, you can now add sexual intercourse to the list of things I won't do in a public bathroom. That list also includes pooping. Dirty.

So, yes, I was getting ridden, while sitting on the seat of a public Porta-Potty, at a county fair. Gross, I know. However, what guy is actually going to stop a girl once she's giving your penis a hug with her minoras? None. It's like when your alarm goes off to get you up for work. You know you should get up, but you can't because your bed is so nice and cozy. Same thing with vaginas. Once you're in, you can't leave.

I really don't know how long I was used as a rocking chair, but it wasn't long enough to exchange DNA. That's because a loud KNOCK KNOCK came through the outhouse door. FUCK. I already knew it was the cops. Don't they know the golden rule of Porta-Pottys? If it's a-rockin', don't come a-knockin'. Somewhat annoyed by this intrusion, I opened the door. Five of them, all glaring at me.

As I walked out the door, still buckling my belt, one of them asked what we were doing in there. Uhhhhh…fucking? Duh. The cop asked for all my information, and I stood there thinking I was definitely getting a ticket for public fornication, or at least indecent something. But he only looked at me and said, "Here's the deal. You're kicked out."

"Of what? This area? As in, the fair?" I replied.

"Correct," said the cop.

They escorted me out without any tickets or ramifications. Awesome. I guess they figured the girl could fend for herself.

Now, I had to traverse back to the hotel in the rain by myself. Easier said than done. I ended up cutting through a construction site, where I fell down a mud hill. When I got up, I am sure I looked like an African-American. No one could have seen anything but my eyes and teeth in the night.

I lurched through the hotel lobby dripping mud everywhere. The front desk didn't appreciate it. I didn't care. I made it to my room, took off all my clothes, and passed out naked in the middle of the floor. My usual classy grand finale.

The next morning, I had no available clothing, so I wrapped a bed sheet around my waist. Two of the girls in our group agreed to drive me home. As we were leaving the hotel, we walked past multiple families eating continental breakfast with their children in the lobby. Could they have asked for a better role model? I can only imagine the discussions I forced those parents to have with their kids. It's probably the same "talk" my dad gave me in middle school: "Son, I don't care what you do, but I don't want to be a grandpa, and you don't want to be a dad." I completely agree, Father. Read you loud and clear.

When I got dropped off at home, my mother was outside on our patio enjoying her breakfast. I enthusiastically waved at her. She just shook her head. At this point in my life it didn't even faze her that her twenty-two-year-old son had been dropped off by two girls at 9:00 a.m. wearing only a bed sheet. Once inside, I hit the couch and started nursing my hangover, until I was rudely interrupted by my cell phone.

It was the Porta-Potty queen. She politely inquired as to how my night ended up. I told her. She then said, "Huh. Well, the police made me go to the hospital. They tried to get me to say you were raping me in the Porta-Potty." UMMMMM, COME AGAIN? That is kind of a serious accusation. "Go to jail" serious. Serious as in "I better flee the country." Serious as in "What the fuck?!"

Before I could choose between heading to see Cousin Canada or Uncle Mexico, she interrupted my train of thought and reassured me that obviously I hadn't done anything wrong and had nothing to worry about. She had straightened it all out with the police, and it was over.

With that, the phone conversation ended, and I calmed down. I took her for her word and decided to drive to Wisconsin for the remainder of the weekend to attend a country festival. I wasn't going to let a little phony rape charge put a damper on my weekend. That would be foolish.

I put the whole incident out of my memory. I partied at the country festival in true Thomas fashion, which meant I was extremely hung over the following Monday. All Monday morning I lay dead on my mother's couch in the basement. What a crazy weekend, eh? All is well. No worries.

I heard the basement door open and figured my mother was bringing me snacks. It was my mother, but there was no lunch in hand. Rather, all she brought me was her patented stern-mother look, and she shouted, "Why the fuck are there two detectives looking for you outside? What the fuck did you do now?" Shit! You know that feeling you get when you see blue and red lights in your rear-view mirror? Multiply that by ten fucking million. All of a sudden, I wasn't hung over anymore. This couldn't be for real.

I'm not 100 percent sure, but I suspect that not too many people have ever had to utter this combination of sentences to their own mother: "Okay. They're probably here because I had sex with a girl in a Porta-Potty at the county fair. They are going to try and say I raped her. I didn't. It was consensual. But that's why they're here."

My mother without hesitation said, "Go hide." God bless her. I calmed her down and reassured her that I had nothing to hide because I wasn't guilty of anything. Thus, I had no reason to not talk to them.

Two female detectives were waiting for me out on the patio. I introduced myself, and we sat down. The first thing I noticed was how hot one of them was. Like, model hot. In hindsight, I should have requested a full body cavity search by her. But I can't really kick myself for that oversight, under the circumstances, rape charge and all. They had me recap my night and then started asking me questions.

By the way they phrased things, I could tell they were trying to paint a really sketchy picture of what happened. I was hounded about every detail for about half an hour. I started getting mad. This was ridiculous. How the hell are they going to try and pin something like this on me? Being white, I always thought I was immune from this kind of treatment from law enforcement. I think I'm going to agree with NWA on this one. "Fuck tha police."

I simply said, "She was on top. She could have hopped off anytime she wanted. I don't get how this is even up for debate, whether or not it was consensual." The detectives explained that a third party had been in an adjoining Porta-Potty and said they heard us having sex and reported one of us may have said the word "no."

Okay. What context was it used in? Apparently, it doesn't matter when, where, or why the word was said. As long as "no" is uttered, the law says it's rape. Wow. So even though both of our stories matched each other, and we both said it was consensual, it didn't matter because someone else may have heard the word "no." That's why I was getting hounded by two cunts. Fucking bullshit.

I'm sorry, but the law's definition of rape is not my definition of rape. My definition of rape is setting up a snare on a jogging path, clubbing in the head like a baby seal whatever gets snagged, and then dragging it back to your cave to have your way with it. Now that's rape. These two detectives were just fishing for a case by asking ridiculous inquiries.

My mother was eavesdropping the whole time and decided this was enough of the detectives' bullshit. She came storming in like the reinforcements for a wounded army, guns a-blazin'. My mother was more intimidating than any of the black chicks who find out who their baby's daddy is on the Murray show. NOT UP IN HERE. I was impressed with the inner hood rat that shone through in my mother that afternoon. "Oh, no, you fucking didn't, bitch."

My mother's tactical onslaught pretty much wrapped up the interview. The detectives left and told me that the investigation was over and I had nothing to worry about. My mother, of course, saved some of her ammo for me once they left. "Can you go one fucking weekend without being a complete dumbass!?" Sorry, Mother dear. I've been told that before, and I'm working on it.

In the end, nothing ever happened from that whole sequence of events. The detectives called the Porta-Potty queen several times wanting her to press charges, and obviously she refused. They had no case. The whole thing was fucked. Consequently, I no longer cooperate with law enforcement.

All in all, I'd say the moral of this story is, don't fuck in a Porta-Potty. Not only is it gross and potentially hazardous to your health, but it's probable you will get a rape charge. I doubt that is your goal in life. Just remember, we have beds, in bedrooms, in private homes, for a reason. I realize it can be hard to remember that. But it is imperative that you don't forget or you will be explaining to your mother why there are two detectives pounding on your door. Trust me on this one.

MADE IN AMERICA

Made in America. What does that phrase mean to you? To me, it means the absolute best. So is that why I titled my book *Made In America*? Do I think it's the absolute best piece of literature ever written? Fuck, no. If we were titling books based on the quality of domestically produced goods, my book would be titled *Made in Zimbabwe*. AKA, absolute shit. The real reason my book is titled *Made In America* is this: the phrase is tattooed on my ass.

One time, when I was really hammered, my friends paid for me to get that little decoration across my right ass cheek. Initially, yes, I was a little upset the next morning. A more sensible person would have waited to make that kind of permanent body alteration at a more appropriate time, such as when they're sober.

However, that initial reaction was just the hangover talking. How could anyone be upset about having the single greatest word ever invented, "AMERICA," forever displayed on one's body? Only communists and terrorists, that's who. And let's make one thing goddamn clear, in case you missed it—I am not one of those cocksuckers.

I love the United States of America. It's the only place in the world where I have the freedom to do as I please. In other parts of the world, the actions described in this book would warrant me a date with a military firing squad. No, thank you. And at times, I think my fellow Americans take their freedom to black out for granted. I'm looking at you, kid who doesn't stand up for the Pledge of Allegiance in high school. You need a swift backhand to your cranium. This is America, goddamnit, and we stand for the Pledge of Allegiance.

We stand because there are millions of Americans who gave their lives so we can freely inebriate ourselves. Otherwise, shitfucks like Bin Laden will try to deprive us of that right.

I can't remember a more joyous day of my life than when I learned that Team 6 finally sent that pathetic piece-of-shit to hell. Watching our military kick his dead body into the ocean to be used as fish food brought tears to my eyes as I chanted "DIE, MOTHERFUCKER" in front of my big screen TV. High definition, of course. America. Fuck, yeah.

Despite the greatness that is the United States, haters talk shit because America gets whatever it wants, whenever it wants. Sorry, rest of the world, get used to it. We've been running this shit since 1776. America makes it rain. Stop hating and accept the fact that America is better than every single other piece of real estate on Earth, and probably the galaxy for that matter.

And because we are superior, we do things our own way. For example, how come we don't use the metric system like the rest of the world? Because that shit is too simple. Sure, it would make a lot more sense to have every unit of measure in increments of ten, but we Americans don't take the easy way out. Plus, it sounds cooler to Edward fortyhands myself than milliliter-hands myself when I'm drinking. So, rest of the world, you can take your Celsius thermometer and shove it up your ass.

Why don't we play soccer, the world's sport? The reason it's the world sport is because anyone can walk out of their hut and kick a cocoanut or rock around. The majority of the world lives in poverty, eats rice, and shits in the same river they drink from. I don't see myself giving up my indoor plumbing or steak dinners anytime soon. So why should I adopt their form of athletics?

Now, I'm not that naive to think that Al Qaeda is sitting in a cave pissed off that I'm in America using a yardstick instead of a meter stick. Every time I turn on the news there is some analyst trying to explain where this anger stems from. They claim it comes from religion, poverty, and American foreign policy. Incorrect. They're thinking about it too hard.

I have the answer. It's simple. While on any given Saturday night I'm enjoying my liberties of drinking beer and creeping out gorgeous women, Al Qaeda is frying in the desert contemplating whether or not they'd rather screw their goat or their wife. Wouldn't you be pissed off having to make that decision?

There's a reason why they make their women cover their entire body with clothing. It's the equivalent of us putting a bag on an ugly girl's head and turning the lights off when you bring her home. I'd probably want to be a suicide bomber, too, if I had to have sex with a Neanderthal who smells like the zoo and has more facial hair than a soldier in the Civil War. The worst part is that with alcohol being against their religion, they have to do it sober. Poor bastards.

Let's just end this War on Terror right now. I have a flawless battle plan. The enemy will be attacked on two fronts: by air and with boots on the ground. The aerial assault will be the standard "shock and awe" campaign. But rather than SCUD missiles, we drop all the *Penthouses* and *Playboys* we can. By the time those fuckers are done gawking over the centerfolds, their hands will be raw.

That's when the boots enter. We send two American television mainstays. We combine the people from *The Swan* and *Celebrity Fit Club* and have them infiltrate every village and cave of known terrorist activity. Once inside, their mission is to make over all the women into Pamela Anderson.

After the cave looks like the set of *Baywatch*, how could the terrorists continue to be pissed off? If a pair of silicon double Ds can't get you to put down your anthrax and RPGs, then you got some issues that modern science can't cure, and we simply go to Plan B with stealth bombers and fry your cave like ants under a magnifying glass. I'm okay either way because I'm going to continue living my patriotic, free, American lifestyle, which is, in case I need to refresh your memory, beer, sex, and parties. I can't maintain that lifestyle anywhere else but in America. And for that, God Bless America. Let Freedom Ring. Because of these freedoms that we all share, I will never get "Made In America" removed from my ass. It will still be on me when I die. And when I die, I will be stuffed by a taxidermist in a position similar to that on the cover of this book so everyone can see "Made In America" for generations to come. And yes, my great-great-grandchildren, you have permission to bring my mount to school for show and tell. You're welcome.

POSTLUDE

I'm sure most of you feel swindled by having forked over any of your hard-earned paycheck to purchase this garbage. I understand your frustration aimed toward me. However, if it makes you feel any better, I too feel swindled. I wasted six months of my life writing this. So can we just call it even? Besides, all purchases are final, and there are absolutely no refunds. So with all due respect, fuck you.

Now that the return policy is fully understood by you, the consumer, let's play book club and reflect on what we have just read. I'll start. f you recall in the prelude, I talked about how I hate books. Well, after writing a book, that outlook has changed. Now, I REALLY hate books. And in all honesty, you should share my sentiment after reading this.

Even though this book intellectually contributes zero benefits to society, I do have several goals that I wish to accomplish through its publication. I've decided to break them into three tiers: global, national, and personal. Even if only one of the tiers gets fulfilled, I will consider this project a success.

Global

The global goal needs many things to fall into place if it has any chance of succeeding: most urgently, Armageddon. I don't care if it's caused by a nuclear holocaust, an asteroid hitting the earth, or a biological plague. It does not matter. I'm not picky. I just need most of humanity and society to be wiped off the planet. Preferably this devastation occurs long after I die.

Why would I want that, you ask? It's simple. Once there are only a few thousand people left in the world who are trying to rebuild society, they will be looking to the past to know how to shape the future. My hope is that the only literature to survive Armageddon is one copy of *Made In America.* Can you imagine people modeling a social structure based on the stories and teachings of "We Festing" or "Party Vallarta"? I probably would have enjoyed Sunday school a hell of a lot more if that were the case. So, future generations, you're welcome.

National

Unlike my global goal, which relies on future and unpredictable events, my national goal is in present time. And so there's no confusion, when I say national, I mean America (the only nation that matters). I don't think that needed to be said, except for the high number of my readers who are required by law to wear a helmet and need further clarification.

For years I've studied artistic expression in rap music. If there's one thing I admire about that culture, it's the "rap battle" or "beef" between artists. Whether it's Biggie vs. Tupac, Jay vs. Nas, or 50 vs. Ja, rappers are always making diss tracks. Since I am not talented (black) enough to express myself through rhyme, my national goal is to start the first author beef. So fuck you, Tucker Max. I single out Tucker Max as the target for my author beef because we touch on similar topics in our writings, and our books inevitably will be compared. But more importantly, I feel he's completely full of shit.

I've read a couple of his stories, and for the most part, the humor (if you can call it that) comes from the dialogue. My problem with this is that if you get "excessively drunk," like you say, Tucker, how do you remember what was said? When asked that on his website, Tucker says he brings a tape recorder when he goes out to parties. BULLSHIT.

So here's my hypothesis. He's either lying about the dialogue, or a big fucking creeper for bringing out a tape recorder. I don't remember during my freshman year of college ever telling my buddies to wait while I rigged up my tape recorder in case I decide to write a book later on in life. It doesn't make sense.

For you diehard Tucker fans who are still clinging to his dick and were rolling your eyes at the previous paragraphs, let me just drop the A-bomb on you. Tucker talks about how outrageous and crazy he is when it comes to drinking and partying, correct? Well, Tucker went to Duke. An Ivy League, private university. That's like finding out your favorite gangsta rapper grew up in the suburbs. I believe the correct phrase is wack as fuck.

So in his opening autobiography, when says he likes to mock posers, he should be mocking himself for looking like a complete asshole. At least he told the truth about that. So again, and I mean this from the bottom of my heart, fuck you, Tucker Max, and your wack-ass stories, too. (If I'm using "wack" in an incorrect context, will one of my five black friends please let me know? Thanks.)

Personal

Since I'm such a humanitarian and thus far have only provided goals for the world and nation, I think a little "me time" is in order. My personal goal is to be able to have zero responsibility once this book is published. I want to be able to go on five-day benders and randomly wake up somewhere and be able to utter this one line: "What country am I in?" That's when you know you've made it.

You see, I'd feel like much less of a loser if I wake up after a binge to find that my yacht is beached on a random island in the Caribbean during low tide, than I would if I woke up naked in the middle of my mother's basement floor. (It's funny how money can make the same party be completely different. In one scenario, I would be awesome, and the other a lame ass, even though I consumed the exact same amount of alcohol.)

But I'm a realist, and I probably will be on the basement floor. A more achievable goal is that I get one or two additional lays per year. Even then, that will only last the next two or three years because after that I will be overweight and burnt out, making me unrecognizable as a bed partner to any females. So if my only return on investment from writing this is that there are four to six more girls I have to buy Plan B for, I'll gladly take it. Heck, I'll even drive them to Planned Parenthood in the morning.

Conclusion

If my "goals" for this project falter, I won't be that bent out of shape. I still remember the day I decided to open up my laptop and begin writing this magical tale. It was after watching the same *SportsCenter* highlights for three hours straight. I thought to myself, Why the fuck am I wasting my life away by playing video games against elementary school kids and watching the same television reruns on a daily basis? Then I said fuck it, and began writing about all the shenanigans that I've gotten myself into the past fifteen years.

Some people may find my humor or life adventures offensive. Fuck you. It's humor, and none of it should be taken literally or seriously. God knows I don't take myself seriously. I truly believe everyone thinks the way I do. It just takes them about ten beers to my sober to say the things that exit my brain.

With that, I hope you enjoyed reading my tales of debauchery because I had twice as much fun engaging in them. You only live once, so I implore you to take a chance on something. I'm going to end this because I'm starting to feel like a coach trying to motivate his team during halftime. I don't like that feeling. Until next time, if you see me at the bar, let's do some shots and try to trick some fatties into coming home with us.

GOD BLESS AMERICA

★

THE END

About the Author

JMF Thomas currently resides in his mother's basement, where he has zero self-sufficiency. This allows him to spend his free time playing games with his kitties and writing his obnoxious stories.

He loves to engage in any activity that allows him to do it under the influence. It does not matter how boring or how suspenseful that activity is. All you have to do is call him up and invite him somewhere. The answer by default is yes. All of his weird and random stories stem from these spontaneous invites.

Because of the randomness of his adventures, it's hard to pinpoint any one place where he will be. There is only one constant in his weekly schedule, and that is him doing laundry every Saturday and Sunday morning from pissing his pants and/or bed from passing out drunk. Someday he hopes to contribute to society, but currently that's only wishful thinking.

www.ingramcontent.com/pod-product-compliance
Lightning Source LLC
Chambersburg PA
CBHW060513030426
42337CB00015B/1881